Dedication

*For each and every soul in Heaven waiting for a name,
and for our most devoted Mother Mary who
loves and cares for these sweetest of angels.*

Acknowledgements

To Fr. Andy Cravalho of The Fathers of Mercy who was first to offer me spiritual guidance with this work. The most difficult step in life—whether facing a trial, challenge, or opportunity—is the first step. Fr. Andy was the hand and heart that walked me through this first big step. I am eternally grateful.

To Fr. Gene Emrisek who was also an early supporter and who has been a constant help. Thank you for your encouragement, your open ears, and your prayers. Your spiritual review has been invaluable to this work, most especially your insistence that the words be published exactly how they were given.

To Fr. Paul Wicker who welcomed this roaming sheep into his flock and who has exhibited the most amazing pastoral heart. I have been nothing less than awed by how you live and minister the message of Christ. Through your belief in the message of this work you have helped enormously in getting this work out. I am grateful for your charitable giving of time, for demonstration of your amazing faith, and for the many, many ways in which your hand has worked to nudge this book across the goal line.

To Laurie Herlihy who radiates grace, kindness, and authenticity from her every pore. You not only shared generously your professional expertise, but, most importantly, your friendship. There were many days you provided me a life jacket.

To Deb Smith who always appeared at the pivotal points in the process; each time offering not only encouragement by her words but, even more so, support by her actions. Deb, I was, and am still, humbled by your genuine caring.

To Janette D. Countess who took on, without even understanding at first what she was really signing up for, the tremendous task of editing this work. I still remember her comment about my "vomiting commas," a moment of humor when I so needed it. I knew pretty much from the beginning that Janette was the right person to edit the book and am just so grateful that she was agreeable. With a most delicate touch, Janette was successful in

WAITING *for a* NAME

WAITING FOR A NAME
ISBN 978-1-4951-1475-5

Editor
Janette D. Countess

Author Photo
Art Sterling

Cover Design
Brian Holdsworth

Interior Design
J.L. Hardesty

Published July 16, 2014
By: IT Media

Printed in the United States by
Thomson-Shore • Dexter, Michigan

Waiting for a Name is a buffet of reflective insights that use marvelous images and plays on words to cleverly and concisely make the argument. So often we use soft words for harsh realities. The author insists on naming what is true; calling a spade a spade. This is most refreshing as it forces the reader to look at the issue with different and open eyes. *Waiting for a Name* is not an easy read. The intensity, depth of reflection, the catchy phrasing and the deep conviction of the author explodes in the reader and, at times, is beyond the capacity of the reader to imbibe more. Overall, a message of hope is proclaimed. We can change our thinking and our actions; and this seems the main motive and objective of *Waiting for a Name*. It is a book well worth the time and effort it takes to read it well.

~ *Gene Emrisek, O.F.M. Cap.*
Mid-America Province of Capuchin Franciscans

Waiting for a Name is written in such a way that any and all current thoughts and issues can be applied, but it also stretches the mind's understanding of Jesus' mission of the cross. This is a book not just to be read, but, more aptly, savored.

~ *Edith M. Gutierrez, Licensed Professional Counselor*

Waiting for a Name will leave you breathless at times, as the words seem to jump off the pages and confront your inner most self. There is no soft serve in the delivery of the truth as the author so brilliantly confronts—head on—the lies of our culture. This book is a treasure of insightfulness and a true "must read."

~ *Deacon Peter M. Schumacher*
Immaculate Conception Catholic Church, Alamogordo, New Mexico; and Founder and President, Shroud Exhibit and Museum

making changes without any change to the words or meaning of the message. Thank you, my friend.

To J. L. Hardesty (Jo Lauter) who has graced this work with her own unique touch by the design of the interior and preparation for print. How we came to meet is a God wink story all its own, and let it be said, for anyone who does not already know, there is no such thing as coincidence. Thank you, lovely Jo, for pouring out so much of your heart and for joining me on this road.

And for various accompanying ways I have also been gifted by, and through, Douglas Clement, Carie Freimuth, Wendy and Allan Cravalho, Jenni Houser, Charlene Feldkamp, Mark Johnson, James Bradley, and Katrina Gelinas. Each of these named persons has touched my life, and, therefore, this work, in a very special way. Each has been an angel, whether or not they even realize.

To my paternal grandparents John Cerny and Blanche Marie Krawczyk and to my maternal grandparents Peter Ambrose Schumacher and Alice Ellen Clink, whom I am certain have offered prayers for me from heaven.

To my parents, John J. Cerny, Jr. and Rita C. Cerny, who have lived so beautifully the vital, precious roles of motherhood and fatherhood. I am most proud not only to call my father "Dad," but also by the title "man" as he is a true defender and protector of his family. My father was the first person to read the manuscript for this book; read at the stage of complete disorder and the greatest puzzle ever. Thank you, Dad. To my Mom, whom I can honestly express is my best friend, I am forever indebted for giving me an assured and safe delivery…albeit a month later than expected. But, hey, who can blame me; even then I had the sense of knowing it's a crazy world. As the words came to me for this book, it was my mother I called to share the inspirations received; many very early morning, nearly daily phone calls. Thank you, Mom.

And finally, with heartfelt love and gratitude for the gift they are, a very special acknowledgement to Jeremiah, Andrew, Jennifer, Elizabeth Ann, Grace, Keith Charles, Diana Marie, Kale, Jean, Annie, Sarah, and Leo. Little ones with feet so precious that, as is true of all in the human family, there can never be, and will never be, another to fill your shoes.

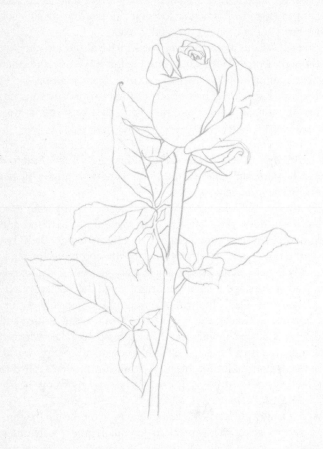

Introduction

*If you have men who will exclude any of God's creatures from
the shelter of compassion and pity, you will have men
who deal likewise with their fellow men.*
— St. Francis of Assisi

What are you holding? Right now, the answer to that question would literally be, "A book." What else might you be holding? Mentally, emotionally, physically, or spiritually, what might you be holding on to? What might you be holding to? This is a different question than the one just previous.

Is there anything holding you back from where you wish to be? What do you hold dear? What holds your attention? Is it time, money, or a particular belief?

Whoever you are, whatever your background, whatever your upbringing, whatever your education, whatever your age, whatever your job, whatever your dreams, whatever your trials, whatever your failures, whatever your successes, whatever whatever, I am glad that you have chosen to pick up and hold this book. I hope that when you lay this book down that the words remain with you; that they not leave you empty handed but rather ignite movement in your mind, heart, and feet.

What is it you hold? You hold the power to love.

Cynthia P. Cerny
June 24, 2014
Feast Day of St. John the Baptist

Chapter ONE

Get a scroll and write.

Maybe the community

will finally get it.

Jeremiah 36:2-3 (MSG)

CHAPTER ONE

*We all know the story of how Herod, alarmed
at some rumor of a mysterious rival, remembered
the wild gesture of the capricious despots of Asia
and ordered a massacre of suspects of the
new generation of the populace.*

G.K. CHESTERTON, THE EVERLASTING MAN

How modern can we trumpet to be over those ancient destroyers who threw men to the lions when in the 21st century men willingly sign over their young to "a procedure" that has no less effect than the jaws of lions? How can we say with any honesty that a cannibal culture of yesteryear is lower than our cannibal culture of this very year when the kettle is so clearly black?

Have we become so small as to claim control over what is so vast that only a sorely rotted intellect could agree to the fallacy? The mentality of the contraceptive crowd is similar to administering poison to a tree to arrest its growth and then later demand abundant, perfect fruitfulness.

Why do we hate ourselves so? Better yet, who is telling the lies? Who is spinning the tales? It is not self-hate you want to admit so you advertise it as self-love and you frame the argument with the weakness of which you feel about yourself. You explain it is not yet the right time, the right person, or the right situation; but, translated, what you are really saying is you are willing to control everything but your own out-of-control desires. You poison yourself and kill all that is inside you. Make no mistake of what you kill. Do you think it is a litter of puppies? No, that cargo you would defend. Human cargo is viewed not worth the carry, least of all defense. You have given the middle finger to what you instinctively know to be true while your mouth proudly declares utter ignorance that a human embryo is merely tissue no more valuable than Kleenex.

Every human life is a human life. It can be no other. A woman cannot birth a dog. Popular culture instructs there to be a magical moment at which point human life begins, which, indeed, is true. The fallacy in this pop culture instruction lies in the fact that it reveres man as the magician, and, in holding to this belief, takes unbridled liberty to revise life's starting marker to the convenience and whim of man's horny magician tendencies and narcissistic needs and so-called rights.

When a laborer encounters a problem on a construction site, he consults the architect, but popular culture has "advanced" to a point of turning against itself in a war of self-destruction

by not seeking the Architect of life. A man and a woman possess the necessary design to come together and perform the act to create a human life, but God alone decides if and when life begins because only God can create a soul. Life begins when God says and God says at the moment of conception, because He designed women not to birth puppies. Simply stated, man has lost taste for God's greatest architecture.

For those who insist that contraception is of no ill effect, they insist with a much twisted imagination. I can empathize. When we apply soft words to harsh realities it can be easy to accept things that a more informed mind, a more clear state, would not elect. Contraception is a contraption which enslaves women and kills the very thing that makes women God's most "very good" creation. A feminist, of course, will disagree. So I have a question for the feminist: What is so freeing about the intake of poison? Do you wish to label me an alarmist? I understand. Truth can be a bitter pill to swallow; we prefer the pill of poison. We will kill; we just won't call it killing.

Chapter
TWO

CHAPTER TWO

Humility is a man's estimation of himself,
according to the truth.

JOSEPH PIEPER, PHILOSOPHER

Pro life. What does that mean? A dog has a life. A cat has a life. In fact, a cat is said to have nine lives. Even a light bulb has a life. So what are we talking about when we talk about pro life? Is it not a child of which we speak? Why then pro life? Should not the questions really be: Are you pro child? Are you pro soul? Might some of us be modern day Pharisees?

Planned parenthood. What does that mean? Is not the truth spoken by the actions of "Planned Parenthood" parenthood prevention? Do you think discipline helps maintain character or erode it?

What do you say it is that you are removing from the womb? Jesus says it is life.

Popular culture sees pro life as an antiquated trait, an obsolete idea. Pro choice sounds more all-encompassing, much less offensive to the easily offended, even though "pro choice" encompasses only half the story. After all, if there is a "pro" there also must be a "con." We need to understand the choice to be made. Is it a child on the table or is it just a woman on the table? If you say "just a woman," then what is her need to be on the table? What is the need for the medical devices? Two very real lives: one named person and one person waiting for a name. Pro or con?

You can deny. You can dig deep and bury bones. Then you can dig even deeper and bury a sad face behind a bright smile. You can pretend. You can spin a situation until you have a weave so tight that nothing can penetrate. You can manipulate words to soften the blow; feed yourself whatever you can stomach. Truth will stand as the only avenue to healing and freedom. Self-prescription may delay symptoms for a month, a year, a decade or even two; but it is no better than an over-the-counter ointment on a third degree burn. What you think you can simply erase you will learn is planted with indelible permanence. The soul that beats in your womb, if only for a few weeks, has forever changed you just as you forever changed that which you failed to name. You were willing to open your legs to a man, but unwilling to open your arms to that man's child. The most you have to offer as a woman, and the most important job you could ever hope to have, you cheated in favor of being a cheap trick.

When you pro choice against life you are, in fact, fighting against your life, as well as the gift of the soul entrusted to you. Your action (or inaction) registers your belief of your inability to fulfill your design. A man is called to provide and defend, a woman called to defend and deliver.

How does your pro choice against the soul give rise to the dignity of the human race? Too broad? How does your pro choice against the soul give rise to man's position over the wild beasts? We do not like when things do not work to our liking. But thinking only of our liking is without thought to what may be an affront to God. It is an interesting argument of the "pro choice against child camp" that the "pro life against death camp" cruelly exploits the single, pregnant woman by attempting to rob her, presumably, of "her body." The argument is appalling and sadly laughable. It is a one-way mirror with a blinding spotlight. There is only one body curled in harm's way of true robbery. It is the precious dignity of the mother that "camp con for wrong choice" dares to exploit: evil exposed. "Death becomes her" is the subtle chant of the "pro choice" that cons these fear-filled women.

What is a man? From the beginning he was protector and provider. One who has not these basic prerequisites may call himself male but should not confuse himself, nor solicit to others that he is a man. It is simple piercing truth that any male who would shield himself behind a woman is too weak to merit a glance.

You don't want to deal with life so you set it apart; you set it in a grave. It is just an added convenience to what is seen as most inconvenient that the solution requires not a hearse but a hiss. In minutes all can be emptied from your womb, avoiding a tomb but never escaping your mind or your heart.

But no one tells you of this unavoidable escape. There is no time to discover life when the place to which you turn is pro to no life. The Nazis played Mozart as life entered gas chambers. Those who are con to life need you to be deaf to a heartbeat when it is your turn to get in line.

Do you think you can keep the secret…from God? The only eyes that matter—God's eyes—want to cry with you. How long will it be before you allow him to forgive you and comfort you? How long before you end the mutual suffering?

We kill babies but we save whales. Many hundreds of human beings are aborted in unmarked offices each day and we do not blink. However, we expect a fireman to enter a burning building and rescue a cat. We murder life but we never see ourselves as the murderer. We claim to own our body but the casket exhumed reveals the fallacy of our claim. It is important to know who owns your body, and I do hope you search for its owner. He is not hiding, and He certainly does not desire to condemn, shame, blame, shout, hurt, criticize or disown you. He simply is waiting to forgive you. He wants to forgive and forget. You see, He already shouldered the load for the soul you chose to sacrifice for one or a dozen reasons; reasons that all added up, basically, to a single word—fear. The One who owns your body, and the One who is owner of the body you were con to deliver, says: Be not afraid. In fact, these very words He speaks over a hundred times, all recorded in a book that someday you may pro choice to read.

Is it not said, even by your own mouth, that it is unnatural for a parent to survive their children? Is it not heart wrenching to know of a mother who lost her child to SIDS, or cancer, or because of a drunk driver, or suicide, or because one morning a classmate was angry. Is it not a devastating loss? The family grieves, friends grieve, a community grieves, and sometimes even a nation grieves. An aborted life, however, is generally not grieved because it is generally not recognized as actual. And it is not seen as actual because it is not seen. Oh sure, it will show on an ultrasound but who wants to look? The beginning of life starts most typically in secret.

Do you pro choice ancient commands or flavor-of-the-day headlines to form your identity? To establish how best to live? Do you find the word "command" too harsh, too restrictive, too unpleasant, or too limited? Does it make your pride swell instead of your heart melt? Is it not omnipotent to know the commander? Is it not omnipotent to know the leader so you may trust and choose rightly? When pride inflates we are following the wrong leader. When apathy takes over we are following the wrong leader. When arguing replaces discussion we are following the wrong leader. When wonderful messages are spoken but aligning action does not materialize along with it we are following the wrong leader. When information is fed that seems almost too easy for digestion we are probably following the wrong leader.

For those who desire the experience of jumping from a plane or propelling from the end of a bungee cord, do they do so with a belief that nothing will catch them, or dare because of a belief that something will? They may take the leap boasting of their bold spirit, but the truth is they merely are daring to surrender. They may boast that the former makes them most human when in reality it is the meekness of the latter that does. Only one who has lost his mind would jump otherwise. And in this example of a jumper lies another secret: In everything we do we are provided a safety net; it awaits us in the surrender.

Honesty is important, but integrity even more so. I think honesty is best described in how you behave when others are witness, and integrity how you behave in secret. And always—always—actions trump words.

You live where you face. Always looking back? In the past then you reside. And since you cannot be in two places at once, would it not be considered wise to be careful in choosing the direction you face? We think we are expert to judge, but do we not perhaps play a part in which we could also receive a sentence? Yes, even those who are pro life. In some cases, could not a valid claim be made that the pro life activists sometimes come across like the Pharisees Jesus encountered? Not all, but some, might benefit from being knocked off their horse. Fear will not approach what is so often viewed as lacking compassion. Fear will not approach what is so often viewed as condemning. Fear will not approach what has already rendered its judgment. Fear is always a cry for mercy.

Never is there a soul delivered to the womb by His hand that is DOA. A woman not in want of a pregnancy is scared and fearful. She is desperate for a plan. Not a plan of attack— either for her or her child—but a plan of support. In the deepest part of a woman's heart she wants a plan in support of motherhood. However, it is normal, because of guilt, shame, isolation, fear, and any other number of negative feelings and attitudes a woman may experience at such a time, for her external communication to speak differently than her internal desire. It is only when a woman is left in the dark from love and truth, and made to believe the only "safe," the only "smart," the only "practical" alternative is to discard her "carry-on," that a woman may be convinced to do what is unnatural.

Guilt, shame, isolation and fear are real and powerful emotions that require compassionate understanding and loving response. One false move and a woman will flee because she feels a burden, not a baby, and her view is utterly desperate. In the case of an unsupportive male, a critical family, well-meaning but misguided friends, and everywhere print and television marketing urging the "nothing wrong" with wiping the womb clean of unplanned "tissue," it takes tremendous courage for a woman not "in want" of a pregnancy to announce to anyone, least herself, the pregnancy. Therefore, when a woman breaks her silence she needs caring ears. She needs the truth, softly conveyed, that peace will not come through breaking away from what has been gifted to her to carry. She needs to know that she is not alone. She needs comfort in what is for her a most uncomfortable situation. She needs safety in a circumstance in which she feels immensely vulnerable. She needs the opportunity to vent her many emotions, not with ready judgment, but with ready arms. She needs privacy to release her secret, not privacy to hide it. She needs reassurance to respond to the *right*, to which her heart whispers against the *wrong* whose loudness is working to shatter her inside with fear, shame, guilt and isolation. She desperately needs love because she has already allowed herself to be used.

Chapter
THREE

CHAPTER THREE

Above all, the common outcry, which is justly made on behalf of human rights—for example, the right to health, to home, to work, to family, to culture—is false and illusory if the right to life, the most basic and fundamental right and the condition for all other personal rights, is not defended with maximum determination.

SAINT JOHN PAUL II

Contraception is the name we have applied to what, in truth, is 21st century child sacrifice. It is pop culture's biggest non-secret secret and something that instead of recognizing with the least bit of horror, we broadcast on television via reminders to "protect" ourselves. Is it not ironic that we use such words as "protection" and "procedure" as a blanket for murder? Does your religion come from the world? Is truth mined from popular opinion and polls? Does your morality change with the seasons? Are you interested in truth or just a way around truth? Do you want truth or false peace? Do you want the whole truth or just the scraps—the cafeteria plan?

The pill was never designed to improve a woman's health; just as it was never designed to prosper families. By utilizing contraception we abandon our greatest protection, turn against our greatest protector—we rebuff heavenly order and pro choice world order. Then we watch cable news and wonder why there is so much pain in the world.

You say: My decision does not affect you. How do you know this to be true? Your child may be the one who is to announce the cure for cancer. Remember, one unrepeatable human; one unrepeatable life plan. Forever could be gone the cure for cancer because your pro choice approves selective killing. Would it not be great, given the truth of the unplanned parenthood mentality, if we could "pro choice" cancer? How arrogant, how selfish, how narrow your vision, how closed your mind, how fearful your action; so fearful that it reverberates around the world. Every aborted child is a death felt so deep in the heart of humanity that, given a name, would shake all that we think we know. You may say I am wrong. You may think I am trying to scare you. Neither accusation will bring peace because neither accusation carries truth. To the former, I am not wrong—every single life affects other lives. And to the latter, it is not I who scares you. That status you achieved by engagement of your own personal behavior.

Is it really any surprise that some people have difficulty recognizing a life that is unseen when they can so easily dismiss life that is standing directly within their sight? However, when an unseen life can be felt and its heartbeat heard, is it not peculiar that we diagnosis the woman with morning sickness instead of morning glory?

You say: Without contraception it would be easy for people to end up with more children than could be manageable. You express concern for not wanting to be the financial support of more welfare mothers and their "too many kids." I find it slightly humorous when someone expresses a concern about being in a "19 Kids and Counting" situation as if it is God who lacks self-control. It is never God who fails; failure is strictly a human area of expertise. And it seems we are always looking for new ways to fail, even extending extra credit points if we can build-in an excuse to blame God in the process.

Your argument for need of "protection" says that the One who creates souls is untrustworthy. It says that humans are not responsible for being irresponsible. It says that we should be able to abuse our bodies against the order of how they have been designed. It says there is a limit to the right number of children and that humans determine that number—not through a relationship of love but through encounters of use.

You say: Children are expensive and you fear that you cannot afford a baby. Whenever focus shifts to "how much kids cost these days," the mind is immediately derailed by the entertainment of debits and credits, and a person is lowered to level of commodity. On the surface, the concern of costs may seem reasonable, even responsible; but that is only because the analysis is one of a partial picture. By dismissing the perfect vision that comes from the higher realm, we blindside ourselves. We profess a need for the protection of contraception because we fail to employ self-control. Grab a calculator and busy yourself running the numbers, just do not forget to account for the 55 million children who have been massacred by "a procedure" that has been approved by citizens of a country that claims to despise killing. And do not forget to factor the cost to our souls—yours and mine—for this killing. Every honest accountant knows it is important that all the numbers add up.

You say: I will have kids when the time is right. To whom does time submit? You say: I know what is best for me. You trust yourself but do not trust He who created you and He who created time. You ask: Is it not prudent to plan one's family? Yes it is, but by whose plan? God has the only perfect plan. God has perfect timing. Yet such wisdom is not convincing enough for the pea rolling and rattling between your ears. You want the role of architect. Watch and see how unnatural one can behave and then how naturally it all ends up in a very fine mess; a brand new reality show.

Planning children is not like car shopping or house shopping. Planning children is not about wanting a girl or wanting a boy; or wanting twins or wanting triplets; or wanting one boy and one girl; or wanting two boys and one girl but wanting the girl to be born first. Planning children is not about wanting children after you buy a house but before summer comes. Planning children is not about wanting children after you secure that better paying job but before you reach age 30.

Does free will have the power to will a child? If "baby making" is merely biology then why is it that a couple cannot always produce a baby after they have pro choiced to want one? In the United States we are working diligently to market "baby making" as something akin to a Ford factory assembly line. When we will to want something; when we pro choice that everything in our I-world is now properly aligned, can we produce a child on our own? It seems we have everything required for the recipe but one thing: the soul. The soul is the main ingredient of the secret family recipe held by our Heavenly Father. You can fight, you can scream, you can deny all you like, but it does not, and will not, change the truth that without God there is no life. God, alone, appoints the breath that starts each heart. If your life is beginning to lose its most beautiful human form, please keep in mind it did not start out that way and it is not meant to end that way.

People say: Why bring a child into the world that is unwanted? Who says the child is unwanted? The male and female who participated in an act of which the primary purpose is to procreate; or God Almighty who alone decides when to bless the act of human procreation? Be assured that as clear as the sun rises in the east, there is no such truth as an unwanted child—our Heavenly Father says so. I believe Him.

What do you say to the single mother with four kids who is already struggling to provide? What do you say to the woman with perhaps a history of abuse by a man or a string of men?

Should it be expected of her to give up the pleasures of sex just because she does not want to run risk of another bad relationship or another pregnancy? Is she not doing the responsible thing by using contraception? Would it not be unrealistic and uncaring to withhold contraception from her?

If you support contraception you are, in truth, advocating that it is best to keep women uneducated. And you, too, prefer to remain uneducated. Look at this from the hard mirror of truth: it is we—you, me, and the single mother—who have gone against the plan of life. It is we who have chosen to rewrite right. You can drain as many pens as you like in your rewrite, but you can never honestly rewrite what has been written in stone.

You say: It is a fair and compassionate decision to end a pregnancy when physical or mental disabilities are known to be a factor. Do you think a mistake was made in the QA department of Heaven? Do you see the pregnancy as something other than a gift just because the gift may challenge and bring discomfort to your established life routine and future prospects? God's ways are not our ways; a fact for which we should be incredibly grateful.

No matter the type or severity of physical or mental afflictions, every child is a child—a soul—chosen and planned by God. We may question His plan, and feelings of concern are certainly human and understandable, but, again, we are not privy to all the evidence. To terminate a pregnancy as some sort of "act of mercy" is a merciless excuse for your own weakness; and perhaps, on some level, a pitiful counterattack to preempt damage you sense will bruise your pride and rattle your well-structured dreams. The child may suffer hardship, but would he not also experience joy? "Joy" not as in trips to Disneyland, but "joy" as in receiving a hug or hearing your voice sing him to sleep. I imagine all the angels in Heaven draw quiet whenever one of these children is gifted; awaiting your response to the simplest of questions: Will you love? How is it you see a life mistake but you do not see a grave mistake?

You say: No woman who finds herself pregnant because of an act of rape should have to suffer through a pregnancy that is nothing more than a reminder of a painful attack she has already endured. I have been a victim of rape. Rape is a horrendous violation of one's body and the rapist should be held wholly accountable for the crime. That said, I can also attest that rape is recoverable to healing. What is not recoverable to healing is death. Despite the serious offense of rape, there is no right transferred that decrees it justified to turn and violate another. To exterminate a child because the scene was one of force by a predator is to yourself become a predator in an eye-for-an-eye seat of judgment. It is a hard truth, but not a truth without compassion. Compassion for two children—you and the one inside you—both deserving of a good, full life.

Imagine you are mentoring a young boy who loves baseball, and you say to him: Son, I want you to play baseball every day. I want you to have numerous turns at bat, but I never want you to hit a homerun. You need to protect yourself from homeruns.

Chapter
FOUR

CHAPTER FOUR

*Modern civilization has raised the material
level of millions of people beyond the expectations
of the past, but has it succeeded
in making people happier?*

William Barrett

A lie is a lie is a lie. And the "I can have it all" mentality is a lie. Some lies you may clearly see as wicked; other lies you may be less inclined to accept for they come from wicked who collect honors for their wonderful lies. People's lives are only as good as their worship. What do you worship? Perhaps you don't like the word "worship." To what do you give most attention? To what do you give most focus? To what do you give most thought? To what do you give most time? Is anything on your list a "who" instead of a "what?" No one can have it all, but I do concede that those who think otherwise certainly have mastered the art of fractured living; fractional existence.

You say: You can have it all. What is this "all" you say can be yours? And, if it is to be believed that there is an "all" possible to possess, when can you be assured you have obtained it and what will be the cost?

You say: Life is short, play hard. However, when we focus on self-pleasure we do not expand as a person, we actually regress; filling the room with self makes for a pygmy ego. It is not that you are unimportant—quite the contrary; it is that you should take care not to become self-important.

Is family more significant than a job? Is family more significant than calculated advantage? Is family more significant than popular opinion? Is faith a risk or do we just not understand the real risk of not having faith? No one who is whole is self-sufficient. We all need someone. It is the easy target who makes it his goal not to need anyone.

Too often we obtain our interpretation of politics, economics and morals from journalists when we should only be gathering information from such sources. The meaning of the world is most accurately given to us by God's Word and demonstrated to us in God's Word made flesh.

If you still desire to reach for the "all" outside yourself in lieu of the "everything" temporarily housing inside you, understand that the price of the deceit of this pro choice is forfeiture of a body and a soul—by untold multiples. We tend to think "having it all" as all benefit and no cost. We think it speaks only to limited desires of finishing school, getting a great job, keeping the boyfriend, etc.; when, in fact, a decision, wrongly chosen and unacknowledged, lives on. Choices removed from body but never soul, never heart, and never mind. But rarely does anyone tell you this when they speak of having it all.

At what age did you buy into the lie that your life is your job? Should a job fit a life or should life be downsized to fit a job? Do you provide for your family or does the hired help? Is "providing" a number or is it more than any number can ever truly cover? What is the "provide" from the father? What is the "provide" from the mother? Frantic is not a pace conducive to nurturing. Hired help, no matter how sweet, is hired help and a heart for hire is no contest for a heart of charity. What is your plan for the day you no longer have a job? What is your plan for the day you no longer have a breath?

What is money? What can money buy? What can money not afford? At what price is one able to secure good health, true friends, close-knit family, freedom, faith, hope and love? Even a list that may entertain your wallet is often reliant upon the gold outside of it; gold from the hearts that built the product, farmed the food, flew the aircraft, taught your child, cleaned your house, serviced your car and protects our shores. Have you not yet learned there are no unimportant jobs? Have you not yet learned there are no unimportant people?

We are becoming masters of the art of disconnection, slaves to technology. Perhaps you remember the advertising slogan, "Reach out and touch someone." The fallacy of this advertisement being that touch cannot be achieved via technology.

Isolation is unhealthy for the mind, and to trick the mind to believe that 836 Facebook friends will prevent one from isolation is only to play the part of a fool. Insecurity feeds from isolation, and isolation feeds from a root fertilized by fear.

We have become inattentively distracted to life and in doing so have torn it to bits and pieces. We work tirelessly only to have become tired. We work frantically only to have made ourselves frantic. We work for aim of many goods forgetting that goods should never been our aim. People should be our aim. Relationships should be our aim. Life and love: that should be our aim. But one cannot know life if one does not know Love. When you look at a Crucifix is it Life or death you see? Look closely and see it is Life with the highest Love.

It is not how many balls a circus performer can juggle, it is the focus placed on each ball. The word burnout did not previously own a definition because the condition did not used to exist. People are not machines and can never operate as machines, so it is cruel and pointless to expect a person to operate against their Owner's manual.

If you insist on doing it all, what have you left for God to do for you? Is it you who holds the key to the door of eternity?

Chapter
FIVE

CHAPTER FIVE

*I can stick artificial flowers on this tree
that will not flower; or I can create the conditions
in which the tree is likely to flower naturally.
I may have to wait longer for my real flowers;
but they are the only true ones.*

JOHN FOWLES

Artificially altering our bodily function does not steady us, it shakes us. On one hand we turn our backs on the organic and clamor for the chemically altered; while on the other hand we clamor for the organic and raise our noses to artificial alternatives. In other words, we value more what will partially waste from our bodies than what can spring from them.

We have so confused ourselves to believe human life is ours to decide whether one should live or one should die. God gave man dominion over the animals, the plants and the fields. We may rightly choose whether a flower remains in the garden or whether it be cut from its stem and adorn our dinner table. We may not rightly choose to eject a human being from its lifeline as we would a flower, a plant, or any other life form. Can you imagine the uproar if we started aborting kittens? The PETA people would go bananas; but there is absolute silence in the face of a life that mirrors their own face. How odd.

When nature rejects one of their own, the zoo keeper comes to rescue. When a woman rejects her own, we tell her everything will be fine. We tell her an after-the-fact pill is best for her. We tell her having "a procedure" is best for her. We tell her many things. We tell her almost everything but the truth, the whole truth. Explain to me how death is best. When every life has a purpose and a plan; when there is no Plan B that can replace a soul, how can death be best? When there is no second string nor pinch hitter who can rightly be called to take over, how can death be best? God has designed a plan for every soul. It is a Plan A only; one-of-a-kind, especially chosen, specifically allocated plan. A plan from God given, but not completed, will always be an incomplete plan, a failed attempt, a void; an abyss, forever on earth a hole. How much do we like it when our plans are altered, most especially by someone with no regard to how it affects us? News flash: It is we who are messing with God's plans. Our plans are imperfect plans. God's plans are perfect plans. Why do we insist on crowning ourselves with a title that imperfect can never in truth hold? We rule what constitutes a human life based on an intellect we do not possess, and refuse the intellect that does. Silly insanity and grave choice (pun intended).

There is a plan for our lives—yours and mine—a specific plan; just like fingerprints. How easily we gloss over this divine fact. Before we left the nest of our mother's womb—no, before we were placed into the nest of our mother's womb—Our Father founded a unique purpose for each of us, and, with His breath to warm and start our heart, embedded this plan into our soul. This "best plan" for our life is a twin gift to our free will. We are slave to no man, nor are we slave to the Divine hand that chose we should be born. Can we even fathom the love?

Some think of God as some sort of prude—anti-intimacy—but nothing could be further from the truth. Fruitful love is conception. Is it any wonder then why we panic when we have perverted the order of love? Conception is a gift. When we sleep around; when our goal is to pleasure ourselves with whomever we like, whenever we like; when we allow ourselves to be used; when we give away the highest treasure we can ever offer another as if it were trash, we know—at our deepest, purest level—we have failed fruitful love. We may have applied the label of love, but we withheld the necessary ingredient of love. Is it any surprise then when we receive a positive pregnancy test we cry foul and demand a do-over? The problem is the "problem" is alive. A do-over can only come at extreme cost; it will cost someone their life.

In choosing to initiate and/or cooperate in sexual intimacy, you signal to the natural and supernatural not a vocation to be a porn star or sex toy but rather a vocation to be a mother (or father, if you are the male participant). Major buzz kill, right? Wrong! It is only man who can take the beautiful that is human intimacy—this most marvelous creative encounter—and denigrate it, mock it, and abort it.

Has your heart ever been broken? What do you suppose we are doing to God's heart? Or does God not have a heart? What is the nothing that keeps haunting you? What is the nothing you are trying to forget but is refusing to go away? What is the nothing you have tried repeatedly to bury but seems always close to the surface? Have you a name for this nothing?

There must be a final choice and the time has come to choose. You choose first; God will choose last.

Chapter
SIX

CHAPTER SIX

The only hope for humanity is Divine Mercy.

Saint John Paul II

God most shows His power by His mercy. How hard is it for you to forgive someone for even a small thing? Wrongs from years ago, even decades, you still reference and harbor with disdain. Jesus, on the other hand, offers Divine Mercy; abundantly yours for the asking. When Jesus forgives, the past is wiped away. Only the moment of now matters. Now is our moment to do better. Right *now* can really, truly be the first day of a new life for you.

God is faithful. He means what He says and says what He means. Do you say what you mean and mean what you say? Do you speak in truth 100 percent of the time, in every moment, of every day, of every week, of every month, of every year? No way! Humans are not angels; although we are capable of demonstrating moments of goodness.

Abraham lied; Jacob cheated; Moses murdered and complained; David committed adultery and murdered; Peter blasphemed and denied Truth. Each of them grieved and each of them received mercy. Forgiveness came on the wings of not expunging these deeds from their eyes, but rather God's willingness to erase it from His. As soon as they accepted clear vision, God could dispatch assistance. God awaited their invite, then cleansed them wholly with His forgiveness and grace.

Are there limits to God's mercy? No! full stop. Only humans place limits on mercy to others, and, most shockingly, limits on God Almighty. Tell me, how is that working for you?

Mercy and truth make for a perfect kiss. You cannot be merciful to someone by lying. Church is not a club. Church is not a shopping center. Church is not a cafeteria. Church is a foundation, and there is only one true, universal Church. He who ordained this church once hung on a tree on Calvary, but now He is risen and He stands next to you. Reach out and He will take your hand.

No sane woman wants to abort her child. Every woman needs protection so that she may, in turn, protect the chosen soul residing in her womb. Society needs real men—not boys in man-aged bodies, but protectors, providers and defenders. Society needs real women—not desperate doormats, but nurturers, protectors and deliverers.

Do you believe your decision back then is unforgivable now or can ever be forgiven in the future? Your action is forgivable. It is worth repeating: Your action is forgivable. There are three people to whom you need to ask forgiveness: 1) God; 2) the "nothing" waiting for a name; and 3) yourself.

Chapter
SEVEN

CHAPTER SEVEN

One looks for an image of man,
attempting in a world increasingly dehumanized
to realize himself as a man ~ to act like a responsible
moral being, not to drift like a mere thing.

Cleanth Brooks

❧

When the feminist says, "It's my body, I can do as I please," she is an opening act for evil. Her actions reveal a truth whose dialogue makes known, "I am like fruit in an open air market. I have been touched by many and put down by many. The experience of this use and rejection, of being handled but not selected, I succumb because who am I to stand on a pedestal?"

Women, we were not born trash receptacles and no man forces us to be so now. Only you can open yourself to things less worthy than you deserve and to less than for which you were made. Ladies, we were made for love—true Love. Fairy tales do come true but true love waits.

So why is it that in bragging to the world that no one may contain you, you have made yourself an easy container for others disposal? What they eject with an attitude of waste from their body you welcome with an inferior attitude of waste into yours.

You run your voice hoarse demanding all your feminist freedoms as you chain yourself to a buffet of addictions. You say: I can stop anytime. Stop does not mean stop and start; it means stop. Stop is an end point, not a pause followed by a restart.

We vandalize our own souls and call that safe. We have lowered our hopes and lessened our convictions. We let loose strong words but then give loosely our body to anyone who will take it, if only for a one-time run or as part of their girlfriend "tryouts." We buy the propaganda and become the pin-up. Do you want to be looked upon by eyes that lust or eyes that love? Do you want to be a repository for many men or a treasure to one?

We are always wanting. We are always ready to use. What can you do for me? Never a line in front of a beggar, but always a line of beggars do we form in front of celebrity. We find the chase thrilling, but how thrilling is it to be used and left behind? You may view yourself as the shopper, but, in fact, you sit on a shelf—rotting merchandise—a cheap display for any matter of male interested in window shopping.

Love can't wait to give; lust can't wait to get. How can life spring from self-centeredness? When one is drunk on his own ego what does he have to offer? Love does not consume, love gives. Takers can never be lovers and lovers can never expel.

Some couples are at ease to announce, "We did it backwards." Such a broadcast most typically refers to having a baby, then living together, and, some time later, having a wedding or common law union. Is this backwardness really such a proud achievement? Just because we can salvage a situation whose starting point is reverse of the Laws of Nature does not make our wrongdoing right. God alone administers grace to cleanse what we pollute.

Would you say this all sounds a bit self-righteous? What is stirring within you to see me as better than you? Are we not both sinners? There is no stage on which I could rightly stand one inch taller than you. I am weak. I stumble and fall many times a day. If you think me to be self-righteous and you only to be attacked, I ask: Why do you choose to be irreverent?

Would you say I am uncomfortable with my body since my choice seems uptight to the feminist expression of freedom? Do you find it unnatural to withhold sex from self, seeing sex as natural, even perhaps a necessity, to good health? Do you fail to accept that we agree to the truth that sex is natural because our agreement does not stay united to the truth that sex is also sacred? In your struggle to see the sacred in sex, you simply accuse me of viewing sex as bad. If you are so comfortable with your body, why do you abuse it? If you want to live naturally, why are you living in opposition to your true nature?

The most dangerous man is the man who does not want to be a man. The most dangerous man is the man who is afraid to live out his role; afraid of what the role requires—not demands, but requires. God is not a dictator; He gives us free will, and He instructs that, with Him, man can fulfill the requirements of manhood. Why else would He have given man the role?

Men of our time are falling like a beetle-infested forest, declaring women wholly responsible for deciding the outcome of the who released from their body. Citing the convenient rationale formulated by women to own their bodies, men today are not a morsel stronger than Adam in the garden who also chose to hide behind a woman as evil tempted and succeeded in stealing life. The serpent which was created spineless made limp man who was created to stand upright. Man was born first for a purpose; to protect and defend. A woman was born second for a purpose; to nurture, defend and deliver. The purpose of the man and the woman cannot be carried out without love, and real love always stands united with God.

Chapter
EIGHT

CHAPTER EIGHT

Faith can wish to understand because it is moved by love for the one upon whom it has bestowed its consent. Love seeks understanding. It wishes to know ever better the one whom it loves… Christian faith can say of itself, I have found love. Yet love for Christ and of one's neighbor for Christ's sake can enjoy stability and consistency only if its deepest motivation is love for the truth. This adds a new aspect to the missionary element: real love of neighbor also desires to give him the deepest thing man needs, namely, knowledge and truth.

POPE BENEDICT XVI

I suspect there are some who consider God a "nice to have," a good standby in a pinch. Why is it that having a relationship with God is to some viewed as odd, and, perhaps, even nonsense? Is it because they think there are multiple gates to Heaven? A front door and a backdoor? Does your My Way Highway end at one of these Heavenly gates? One of the few things we are intolerant of today is God. Mr. Buzz Kill. Mr. Meanie. Mr. Boring. Mr. Outdated. Mr. Strong Arm. Mr. Control Freak. We condemn what we don't understand. We want an explanation for everything; an explanation, that is, which satisfies our drunken prideful egos. Should an answer be elusive or anywhere outside the self-painted portrait of our I-world, we tend to flex to making up our own rules as we go along.

Where is the scientist who could force the moon to remain on duty if the sun failed to report to work? Where is the physician who can construct a soul? Where is the politician who can re-make the world? Where would you turn if everything and everyone turned on you? Would your head drop or would your knees bend? Do you not see that in your stubbornness your knees are already bent? In fighting what is natural by Divine design, you have fallen flush with the ground. The snake will stop at nothing to bring you to his level, justifying the feelings of all your wrong actions in such a way that the cherry flavor hides the poison well. We have grown used to dilution, to dissolution, to a watering down of lies from leaders we should not follow, to pressure from mobs we should not join.

Spoon fed, we seem to find comfort. We hardly give thought to the hand holding the spoon. We give even less thought to what is held on the spoon. We eat as a slave, but no slave is served from a silver spoon and only a fool believes tin to be silver. Are you slave or fool?

Faith is being obedient to what God has revealed to be true. Faith is not us setting our own agenda for what we may wish to be true. God can neither deceive nor be deceived. The question of faith, therefore, is whether you will surrender to what God has revealed to be true or whether you will surrender to the consequences of truths of your own fashion.

Rootless relativism says, "That may work for you, but it's not for me." Rootless relativism says, "That may suit you, but it does not suit me." Just where are you shopping for your suit?

If one is out of touch with reality; if one does not operate on the basis of objective evidences, but wishes only to feed from one's own desires, emotions, and will—that is rootless relativism. It is you who designates yourself god. You design the crown and you make it to fit your head. How is that working for you? It is a dark, dangerous road for the off-roaders; everyone commanding their own little kingdom of diversity. Diversity that really is not diverse at all; at least not in any healthy term.

Some say it is not a consistent world in which we walk, but the fact is there are consistencies in this inconsistent world. The sun rises in the east and sets in the west. A rainbow follows a heavy rain. There is a spring, a summer, an autumn and a winter. A clock ticks to a 24-hour-day. No matter what man may wish to change about these consistencies to render them inconsistent he would be dealing against a higher hand. The Creator was present at creation, not you.

What is your center point? Who is your center point? Does your long-range plan—does your long-term goal—stop at your grave marker? Is there more than your visible life? How do you wrap your arms around eternity? Think of the cross stretching north and south, stretching east and west; where does it end?

Chapter NINE

CHAPTER NINE

The difference between the right word
and the almost right word, is the difference
between lightning and a lightning bug.

MARK TWAIN

You say you own your body. Do you also own your soul? Are you creator of your body or curator of your body? What is it, exactly, that you own? The egg released? The sperm discharged? Is it not a heartbeat that signals to open ears the start of a nine-month countdown? Who starts this heart beating? An egg is a monthly traveler, sperm will ejaculate at any invitation, but a heartbeat is planned.

How, exactly, did you obtain ownership of your body? With whom did you consult in making the purchase? By what proof do you hold ownership? Just where did you go and with whom did you negotiate to own your body?

How is it that you awoke this morning? Is it by self-determination that your eye lids function? Is it by self-power that your eyes are exposed to light and not blindness? Where do you go each morning to purchase the new day? Is the calendar which shows there to be 12 months to this year, a guarantee that you will experience each of these months? Show the receipt you hold to prove ownership of the coming

24 hours, or even just the next 60 minutes. Perhaps it is filed in the same box where you have stored evidence that you also own your body.

To own is to possess. To possess is to control. Do you wholly control your body? Are you able to fight off all illness and disease? Are you invincible to injury? If you own your body then, by default, you must own everything that makes up your body; every single cell of every body part. But what about what is invisible to your body? Do you have ownership of your thoughts? Do you have ownership of the pictures taken with your eyes? Do you have ownership of your experiences? Do you have ownership of your soul? Do you have ownership of the soul inside your womb?

If you own what is inside your womb, were you not once in a womb? Where is your owner? By your own argument, have you not already been spoken for; must you not belong to someone other than yourself?

What we own is free will, and each of us will be held personally accountable for our choices ~ both pro and con.

Chapter
TEN

CHAPTER TEN

Nature, including human nature,
will not bear any absolute and sustained contradiction.
She must be converted, not outraged.

UNKNOWN

You say what is true for me may or may not be true for you. Do you not understand this is impossible? By definition, truth is truth. It is only one thing. To be more than one thing you would have to tag it a variation of truth, a half-truth, a partial truth. When you allow situations to be painted freely outside the lines, it is dangerously easy to be swayed and become bent by any variety of ideologies and philosophies. It is vital to be anchored to a solid base rooted in truth. I knew I was right until I found out I was wrong.

Ask yourself, is it conscious speaking or is it opinion speaking? Conscious is from God; opinion from our picking and rejecting—the ultimate in human cafeteria plans; self-service at its worst. Why do you strive so hard to be agreeable with everyone but God? Did you know that the second largest church in America is non-practicing Catholics?

When living a life of distraction and self-indulgence we live a very small life. Living in an I-world can feel good and comfortable for a long time because it requires no heavy lifting, no long distance running, short-term memory, poor eye sight, poor hearing and a very short reach. It is cocoon-style living with no desire to go beyond. You subsist under the headline "Play Hard," and you are perturbed by anyone who may not have seen the headline and recognized your picture. No one is going to tell you what to do with your body, you brag; which is such an interesting argument given: 1) the body in question—the one in which your soul resides—you do not own; and 2) in the situation of abortion, the choice and action to abort trespasses into territory of which you hold no rightful authority and victimizes another body—a body with a heartbeat, a soul and free will. You do not possess the child growing inside your womb; you house the child inside your womb. The womb is, by design, made to deliver; it is not designed for retention nor is it designed for death.

It is by selfish ignorance that a woman claims to own what she does not hold deed and never will. Most alarmingly, there is an ever-growing audience siding with women who declare the womb to be enemy territory, and these silly suffering egos disparage anyone who would dare comment on behalf of, or offer support for, the life curled up alone and exposed on the battlefield. These poor, desolate minds register "judgment;" without openness to understanding it is not contempt of the woman, but esteem for the child. It is not judgment that is needed in any case, it is an alarm clock. I do not condemn these women to death, just as I do not want them to condemn others to death. If they want to be responsible for their body (which is the best anyone can do given ownership is not possible) then they need to stop giving their body away. Self-control and self-discipline brings great freedom. If women feel they really must own something I would hope them to own the truth.

Will following a crowd escort you to truth? Maybe. Maybe not. The truth is not always popular and the popular are not always truthful. Truth requires strenuous personal participation. You may have heard the saying, "Something got lost in the crowd." That something lost is often the truth. It is not a one-time archeological dig; it is a constant centering, a life-time schooling because we tend to have the attention and retention of a two-year-old.

Have you ever had a conversation with someone with whom you concluded, "He's one of those religious types?" What do you mean when you label someone "religious?" If a doctor were to draw blood from someone you thought "religious" and then draw blood from you, what might the test results reveal about either of you? What about a case where one person owned six vehicles in their lifetime and another person only three. Does such information define either of them in any substantive way? "Religious" has become an association many wish to avoid not because the word is bad but because of the serious distortion of its true meaning; what it has been rendered to "look" like.

You demand tolerance of others but when tolerance is asked of you, you balk. Only God is truly tolerant. He allows us free will. He allows us to walk wherever we choose, speak however we choose, believe whatever we choose, and act however we choose—right here, on earth. Heaven, my friends, is another story. Heaven is the "happily-ever-after story" where His will shall be done; His justice served; His truth triumphant. His all-conquering love will conquer all. What you choose now matters now and will also matter later; it is called eternity. You think you are your own person. God thinks you are His child. How you choose to apply your free will will impact whether your personal story ends happily-ever-after or whether it just ends.

The agenda of our daily lives is composed not so much of places, things and tasks, but primarily of named persons. We are not labels or groups; we are persons with names; names that fear to be judged. Places, things and tasks are toothless to administer judgment. Named persons, on the other hand, very often confuse the prudent exercise of discernment with the unjust exercise of making decree against a soul of which they have no entrance to examine their heart, let alone the depth and breadth of their life experience to date. It is God's job alone to judge and to deliver justice. No human life is without value. Even a bad example is useful; even extraordinarily useful. Until a person stops breathing there is opportunity and invitation to turn their life around to be and do better. There is also opportunity for a person to continue to find ways to avoid what is right, continue to sin and behave irresponsibly. But, please understand, we—you and me—will also be held personally accountable when our name is called. When our Heavenly Father calls us home, will our actions show we were loyal to Him, or, by pro choice, loyal to the way of self and loyal to the way of the mob?

Ask yourself: Who do I want to make of myself and with what do I have to work? Notice, the question asks who to make of yourself; not what to make of yourself. You are a who, a named person, you are a one-of-kind, irreplaceable person, and you hold an immeasurable part in the happily-ever-after-story—for your family, your neighborhood, your work, your community, your state, your country and this world. Yes, high expectations; and each of us needs to become human to reach this high bar. What I mean by this is that we need to stop acting worse than animals; we need to stop killing the heart that beats in the womb.

Women need to own up and men need to step up—defend, protect, and deliver life, not death. We must realize we are dealing with persons, persons waiting for a name.

God's plan is that every soul be delivered. Is it your plan that His plan should be aborted?

Deafness caused by fingers jammed into our ears. Blindness caused by cold hands pressed hard against our heart. Fear of light gives way to darkness and darkness weighs against acceptance of light. Free will. Do you understand the weightiness of this divine gift? It can be released to be as carefree as the birds of the sky or it can be anchored as a ship rotting on the ocean floor. Free will. Turn it around: will free. How do the words speak to you now? Has the exercise of your will elevated you or chained you? Why do you run from freedom? Freedom flies; it does not walk, it does not run, it does not crawl.

Blind instinct. We hold the blinders; God's hand sets the seed of instinct. Free will. To whom will you listen? To what or whom will you turn? To what or whom will you turn away?

Contrary to the sermon of pop culture, we are born with an instruction manual. It is just that we do not own the instruction; God is our instructor. God is owner of the manual which he most personally composed for you and for me. Like snowflakes and fingerprints, no two souls alike.

Imagine a mother who patiently teaches her child to walk. The child, based on the mother's instruction and encouragement, trusts that walking is right and good. Now, consider if that child thought crawling best and elected to forego walking and stay close to the ground instead of trust the instruction of his mother. We are like the toddler who thinks he knows best, choosing to crawl. Then we are dumbfounded when we cannot see the feast on the table. We have elected crumbs because we have elected to crown ourselves superior to anything taller than ourselves.

Think yourself as a lifeless limb on a tree—a dead branch. It is by your free will that you have chosen. A limb which is dried up because it no longer feeds from the healthy part will snap like the twig that it is and drop away as member from the rooted body. A limb which feeds from a healthy root is unable to be snapped as a lifeless limb. Therefore, for a healthy limb to be disconnected from its larger part, the feeding limb must be pulled and tugged; twisted and mangled; mutilated and strangled. When a living branch is separated from its source of dependence, it leaves behind a trail of interior fluid—tears of its tearing and its separation.

We—you and me—have been given a great voice by the One who created us. This voice is free will. It is ours to exercise onto self, but none other than to self. A body, although inside of us is not a body within us. We reserve only the obligation and duty to protect that body. And this body, which could not exist without a soul, but whose soul can exist without the body, is determined and placed by God. In other words, a woman's body is her own but a body inside of a woman's body is not solely hers alone. She owns not its soul. Therefore, judge and executioner she should not proclaim nor act, but only the strongest, ardent, courageous protector of all outside of her inside. God's will, not hers, be done. Or to state it most simply, life over death be conqueror.

Does a woman who chooses to have what is living within her be torn from her without effect? Even the smallest of bandages removed from a cut is felt. How much more so you cannot even begin to imagine from an interior hole, tied forever to your heart, against its free will and its plan for the world.

A mother never forgets her child. Never. A mother is your title because a child is the body that was inside, no matter how small. Even Horton heard a who.

Chapter
ELEVEN

CHAPTER ELEVEN

An intelligent, discreet, and pious young woman is worth
more than all the money in the world. Tell her that you
love her more than your own life, because this present life
is nothing, and that your only hope is that the two of you
pass through this life in such a way that in the world to
come, you will be united in perfect love.

ST. JOHN CHRYSOSTOM

What is your name? Who gave you this name? When were
you given your name? Does the latter question seem silly to
you? Let me ask another: Might you have another name? A
name bestowed by the One who cradled you before your
mother? When was this name given you and who was it that
spoke on your behalf? In other words, when were you chosen;
first recognized for being you? If we are not recognized, how
is it we can go home? Your parents named you at your birth;
God named you at His drawing board. One name registered
in the world; one name registered for all eternity. Both names
certified by doctors—one human, one Most Holy.

What does it mean to be a woman? Look at the beauty and
detail with which you were made. What clues are there that
communicate a womb is designed as a safe haven, a nurturing

place and not a battlefield? A mama bear protects her young; she does not offer them up to predators. It is her design to protect that which is a part of her by instinct and reality. Does a woman have less than a mama bear instinct? Certainly not. A woman knows intuitively and consciously of her amazing capacity to deliver life.

It is a woman in fear, feeling unsupported, unloved, alone, and experiencing the powerful emotional cocktail of shame, guilt, desperation, and isolation, who needs the embrace of love. Love does not say to her that she deserves to have it all and that "this situation" is no part of the "all" she deserves. Love is not siding with her fear as she unleashes her own free will to war with the free will of the one who is months shy of a cry although not one second short of his life's plan. Love's action is hope, even though the woman's free will may accommodate failure as an option. And is it not this very failure of women in America that has become our most fervent national anthem; a defense that defends no one. If we are ever to be truthful, if we are ever to re-establish love of children, we must at least acknowledge the sound of a death march.

Adam named each of the animals; but men and women today deny dignity to even their own offspring by refusing to give what even the animals have: a name. What we treat as impersonal will become impersonal no matter how personal it may be in truth. What is a pregnancy? A blessing? A curse? What is a birth? A gift? A punishment? To know a person you must have knowledge of that person. To know a person is to love a person because you cannot love someone without knowledge. How many tears to fill an ocean?

When you see a child does not everything change? One can hardly help but smile; many even change their speech. Why then do we dismiss before our eyes can see? Why are we negative to what is positive? Why do we hope to kill and kill hope? What do you do by refusal to name: reduce a role; melt into a cultural trend; run with the mob? And is this not just for starters and the least benign? Are you stuck in a life of maybe?

What is the first thing formed of a person? The heart. Where does the soul house? The heart. What then is life?

There is much debate over the time date that marks a fetus a baby. Where is the debate over the time date that marks a pregnancy? We have no problem stating that a woman is pregnant; just look at all the "crisis pregnancy centers." Why is it that we accept so easily a pregnant woman but cannot accept without the greatest of difficulty with what she is pregnant?

If it is not life developing inside the woman then no procedure would be necessary. So what name dare we give it? "Procedure" is vague enough to be comfortable; harmless enough to ask for a sip of the Kool-Aid. Surgery? Surgery to cure what? Operation? Operation to repair what? A life that is growing can be nothing other than harmed by the free will decision of a procedure, a surgery or an operation. So what name dare you give it?

How small is a soul? What is its measurement? What is its date stamp? When does a soul come alive? A life—no matter the size—is a life. To what size does a mustard seed grow? To what size are the plans God has designed for the seed inside you?

God entrusted a woman—Mary—to bring forth His Son. It was the woman God entrusted to deliver. Whoa! Do you not understand the omnipotence of the delivery? How upset you would be if the U.S. Postal Service failed to deliver your $387 million Lotto check? Compare that to a woman who fails to deliver a child. Money is finite, it can only go so far and last so long; but a soul is created for eternity. Even if you pro choice to escape your responsibility as the mother person or the father person, God honors this abandoned person. While you stand behind the rules and prerogatives of a job description (self-proclaimed owner of your own body) to do work that destroys what you dare not name, God's love names.

Unwed mothers? No, just mothers. We must stop with the adjectives. If we want to kill, perhaps we should kill the label maker and raise our voices to the truth. "Mother" is a pronoun—today, tomorrow, and always. "Mother" requires no adjective; the name stands beautifully as is.

Who takes care of the mother? Who loves the mother? The child loves the mother. God loves the mother. Mary watched as her son was murdered, and we continue to subject her eyes to the murder of more of her sons and daughters. How much can one mother take?

Chapter
TWELVE

CHAPTER TWELVE

How many a man is proud of the woolen cloak
on his back, not remembering that it was
on a sheep's back before it was on his.

SAINT THOMAS MORE

We say we want to be original. Every generation tries hard to break molds in search of originality. Recent generations have tried tattoos and body piercings, gothic dress, long hair, neon colored hair, and droopy pants. What is so comical about all such demonstrations is the utter and thorough absence of originality. The key to originality—and, frankly, the only way to be original—is to live the life God specifically designed for you. If you are serious about wanting to be original, follow God.

We talk about how we want to be original, but then we act against our original design. Each of us is born original. You are purely original from the moment of the first beat of your heart, and the first beat of any human heart takes place inside a womb. It is only by living in opposition of our originality—buying lies written on billboards instead of truths etched in stone—that we become poor copies, faux characters of a character that will claim to lead us on a path to having it all, only to find at the end mere crumbs that have cost us everything. "All" is never, and can never, be outside you. So to what "all" will you direct your free will? Might I suggest you look not to the all but to the Almighty.

We like to display multi-faceted sides, but we cannot find peace wearing a public face and a private face. Each of us has only one true face if we dare be who we are. Actions frame character and character is fueled by substance. Both begin in secret but end within judgment of universal eyes.

We are always searching to answer who we think we should become, instead of asking who God wants us to be. We do this mostly because He has high expectations and there is suffering involved, suffering of surrender. But, in truth, surrender is the key to avoid suffering in the sense of pain that is unbearable.

You have to name it to own it, or do you? And is that not the problem? Who wants to be owner? Who wants to declare ownership? We fool ourselves by thinking if we deny, it will disappear. But denial is merely a situation in hiding; hiding in a place that can never be concealed. Eventually what we deny appears, or, more accurately, re-appears. The only question is: What form is the reappearance? Is it addiction (the full menu of); physical ailment; despair; anger; serial relationships; weight challenges; or something else?

If we choose only to listen to the sound of our own voice or to the sound of the many voices around us, how do we suppose we can ever achieve a deeper, better status of living? We need to listen to the highest voice, the voice of truth that whispers not shouts. The voice that is often difficult to hear and even more difficult to follow, but only by manner that we do not always like the simple starkness that truth speaks or the rough terrain that truth requires we climb. Many say life is not easy but perhaps that is because they believe themselves to be captain, crew and passenger. They believe themselves to be the answer to every question and solution to every storm.

Don't concern yourself with gratifying your desires; concern yourself with gratifying your duty. Yes, it is an unpopular message. It is the message that divides the meat from the filler; the men from the boys; courage from the cowardice; life from death. Mindless or mindful? Get and consume or give and reap?

Who do you think you are? To answer this it may be easier to consider who you are not. You are not your weight or your height. You are not your education or your job title. You are not your home address or your recreational talents. You are not your successes or your failures. You are not the color of your eyes, hair or skin. You are not the money you have sitting in a bank or the kind of transport you have parked at the curb. You are not your physical or mental strengths or challenges. You are not your political ideology or your discerning social views. So then, who are you? Are you not more than the face in the mirror? What of the character in your heart? You are not only what moves your body but also what moves your soul. We are actually too much for our own eyes to see. Life is that true, that deep, that profound, that precious. We can live our whole lives and, sadly, barely get past the surface, even with those closest to us. We worry so much about being accepted that we often cloud the truth that the only eyes that matter in this world, and in the world we cannot see, long ago accepted us and will not turn away.

When you see a husband and wife together do you think "rut?" Do you wonder how they could possibly be happy spending year after year together; for one decade or two, or, my goodness, five decades or more? Do you see indifference instead of purpose? Do you see boredom instead of thrill? Do you see labor instead of fun? Perhaps you have even convinced yourself that such living is unnatural. You might accept that a long, long time ago it was okay to have only one mate "forever" because people died young. How can we think it normal that modern people with life expectancies of 80 or 90 years commit to just one person? The answer is very simple: it is the blueprint. You can use a 2x4 in construction when the plan calls for a steel beam, but the result will not prove sturdy; and someone—or some bodies—may be seriously harmed.

Your mind needs higher schooling if it is to pass the entrance exam. If you already claim to be the teacher how will you ever open to the role of student? If you believe in shortcut solutions how can there be room in your head for expansion? It is ironic how we can so foolishly and splendidly distort life, never bothering to see if the bottom line ever adds up. When we go from this person to that person in an attempt to satisfy our desire for sex under whatever banner we elect to fly, are we not less than a wild ass? They sniff the wind for the scent of a mate in accordance with their blueprint. Our noses snub our glorious design. We can't even imitate an ass with credibility. We jump from one lover to another, never loving. We use and then dispose. We treat one another with little to no regard. We take and then dump. We call it love when it is pain we dispense: lover libel. We were not meant to live in emptiness; we were meant to live in fullness. Fullness of love. Love is our purpose. So why do we insist on accepting use? Why do we act like the ass?

Chapter THIRTEEN

CHAPTER THIRTEEN

What is irreplaceable if not time and people?

❧

No doubt you have heard it said: Time is money. Time is time, period. If we are so compelled to re-brand time, I suggest we brand it a gift. Time is a gift. Time is a gift of which we are receivers and which, in turn, we may choose to spend our portion with others. Contrary to the popular phrase, we do not make time. And contrary to an even more popular phrase, there is no such reality as quality time. These are human tag lines, although they seem to make some of us feel better; more in control. However, as with all advertising, it may benefit us to recall the axiom: Buyer beware. Such seemingly benign messaging can wreak havoc on the message and eventually lead where it is not good to go. Stop and think: I will make time. What are you really meaning to say? I suggest it has nothing to do with "making" time and everything to do with ordering your day. You cannot add one minute to the world's clock nor subtract one second from the 60; but you can establish order in that singular spin around the dial. The source of time is God, and within each of our hearts He has appointed a time. Truly, a time to live and a time to die. His will sets the time, but human free will may activate the snooze feature or otherwise interrupt and disconnect the dial. Have you ever said to yourself in regard to your significant other or child, "I will spend quality time with them tomorrow?" Do you believe there is time of lesser quality? Do you believe time requires some level of formal preparation and planning before it is fit to spend with quality? How does one divide that which cannot be seen, cannot be touched, and cannot be banked? "Quality" by whose definition? "Quality" by whose sum?

We live as if we have no real place to go. We rush to do this and that with an ever-changing center point. We find it hard to slow down. We work on just about everything except the one thing that matters at the end of the day, and the end of all days: relationships.

We enter dangerous territory when we do not allow for silence; time for quiet contemplation and reflection. We were meant to run but we were also meant to rest. And not run until made to rest but run in rhythm with restful time. The best choices are not made under stress. It is foolish to count on our best performance being delivered under pressure, even if we can occasionally "pull it off." Standing with the mob and reciting lines from a script to gain "approval of the moment," is far different and a lot easier than working out a life of justice and love among the people you work and live with. Is there a practice to your daily life or just a schedule? If we are so busy working to keep up living on a basis of outward appearances why should it surprise anyone to have no feel, no sense, no belief in any inward reality? Image vs. substance. Propaganda vs. truth. Wrong vs. right. Evil vs. good. We like images, but we don't like to look too close or too long. Focused too long, our eyes become bored. Focused too close, we may be exposed to something hard to absorb. When you really like a particular food it is easy to overeat, even to the point of upsetting your digestive track. However, when served something not to your liking, no matter how good it may be for you, it is easy to push it away and say "No thanks, I am full."

We want fast and furious. Not because we were designed for that but because we have trained for that. We have made it our practice. We like to brag about being in control but often our behavior demonstrates a complete lack of control. Feel free to play twister with your words until you are bored with your own voice and convinced by your own confusion. The truth shall always remain standing: sexual intimacy outside of marital relationship is the epitome of no self-control.

We are so plugged in that we are becoming completely unplugged; sorely disconnected. If we are not walking with God we are not walking, we are crawling. Many of us are so busy rushing from here to there that, at the end of a day, we can hardly even recall what happened. We are living a blurred existence. We go from sleepwalker to chaotic to machine. If we are always in a rush—always bouncing from one activity to another—responding to demand after demand, how is there time to develop anything? Where is the leisure to reflect on anything, let alone anyone? Given modern technology and current conveniences, why does it seem that life is ever more complicated? Where is the stress reduction? Where is stored the deposit from all these time-saving products and processes? Why is there more of a need to rush? To what purpose? Who will know if we ever lived if only for self we live?

Chapter
FOURTEEN

CHAPTER FOURTEEN

Who do you think is readier?
God to give joy or you to receive it?
BROTHER GILES

❧

Conscious versus opinion. Imagine you have the window seat in a 787. The aircraft takes off and as it climbs it reaches an elevation or age, if you will, where storm clouds may present themselves. Soon the landscape below disappears and you are encased in chaos. It can be overwhelming without reliance on something more than the mind, as the mind can play tricks on the senses. This is when an instrument panel can be a reliable "turn to." How secure would you feel if the pilot chose, in the midst of mountainous terrain, a heavy blanket of swirling darkness and angry air, to forego the instrument panel and "wing it" because, well, he just felt like it. The pilot would be exercising restricted vision with unbridled pride and arrogance—a good flight plan if you are in want of a crash landing. God sees everything. Nothing slips His radar undetected. Nothing. If you want to play football with God, understand it is impossible to throw him a fake pass. But He, for His part, will never cease to pull you up from the bottom of the pile for as many times as you desire to attempt another play. God knows the blue sky that is painted above the darkest, scariest threats. All He asks is that you trust that the blue is there and that He knows the best way for you to maneuver with least turbulence, most peace. God, in this sense, is our instrument panel and you can truly fly on eagles wings if you choose.

Worry is weight; surrender is soaring. Opinion is self-reliance; conscious is soul reliance. Self is more than body and clay for there is also a soul, and soul is of God and spirit. Where is it you can find rest? Worry is no small thing and it is advantageous to be aware when it attempts to deter our path. Worry is like hurdles on a track. If we allow ourselves to focus on worries—these hurdles—we immediately become blind to the open space in the lane off to the side that permits us to simply walk around. We do not need to take control; we only need to take a hand. And does it not follow that the hand holding the safest plan for travel would be the hand that actually designed the original landscape. But do not be fooled, "safe" does not denote without sacrifice. Why would it when love cannot exist without sacrifice?

The word "sacrifice" tends to make us cringe because the natural tendency of our material world and our self-centered attitude is to interpret sacrifice as a bad thing. In the case of love, however, self-sacrifice—mutual self-sacrifice—is a thing of splendor. Choice is a negation and negation is a sacrifice. When a man sets his heart upon a woman and asks her to marry him, he is not only making the declaration that "I choose you;" he is simultaneously declaring "I reject all others; I choose you and you only." And the woman, in accepting the man's love, makes the same declaration; she rejects all other men for the heart of her beloved.

Love is sacrifice—it's that rooted, that difficult, that beautiful, that secure, that obedient, that faithful, that divine. There is no shortcut to love. There is no denying love. It is or it is not. You cannot be "in the middle" with love. There is no neutral when love is involved. It is all or it is nothing. Ask a mother when her newborn hungers if she is neutral to respond. Love does not speak one direction then turn and walk in the other. Love is hard! We are not good at loving, but loving is what we are called to do. In fact, loving is why we were made. The fact that loving is hard, it is difficult, it is painful, it "costs us," it requires work, is not an acceptable excuse not to love. Were you just able to ride a bicycle? Were you just able to snowboard? Were you just able to play a musical instrument? Or did you have to learn? Did you experience overnight success or did it require dedication, commitment, desire, hard work, tenacity, and practice to improve and perfect? Who taught you? Did you seek out an expert swimmer to teach you bass guitar? Did you ask a hockey player to instruct you in ballet? Probably not. Then why would you not go to Love to teach you how to love? What can you possibly learn about love from contraception other than contraception is not love; contraception is the graveyard of love. You may hate the way that sounds; I agree with you as I don't much care for it either.

But we must not trick our ears. We must not confuse silence that is death with silence that is peace. There is no such thing as buried treasure; you give life to what you treasure.

Chapter
FIFTEEN

CHAPTER FIFTEEN

*There is nothing in life that is to be feared
but offending God.*

SAINT JOHN CHRYSOSTOM

If we cannot agree on what is human life, how can anything else be relevant? How can anything else matter? How can anything else change? How can anything else be cherished? How can anything else be saved? We should not be assessed for our economic potential or deprivation of our stock portfolio. We have to receive a name by others as that is part of the process of being fully born.

The personal name—your name—is the most important part of speech in our language. The unique spirit in contrast to generalization and grouping, or, worse, a spit wad aimed at God. Naming focuses the essential and has enormous significance.

Eugen Rosenstock-Huessy has scrutinized the meaning of naming: "The name is the state of speech in which we do not speak of people or things or values, but in which we speak to people, things, and values... The name is the right address of a person under which he or she will respond. The original meaning of language was this very fact that it could be used to make people respond."

It is my body, my decision. Of course you may think that, but that is only admitting to yourself half the story. There is another body and there is another soul involved. You are entitled to raise your voice, but you must raise it for two and you must hold firm for whom you speak and by what authority you speak.

At our birth we are named, not numbered. At our death should we not also be named? Or will a mass, unmarked grave suffice as it did in other holocausts of earlier generations. Skeletons of human beings then; skeletons of human beings now. Stalin and Mao and Hitler robbed many of human status; they denied them name, recognition, and life. "They" simply did not fit their plan. You do not see a human in your body either so you, also, deny a name, recognition and life. "It" simply does not fit your plan.

Let us recall another such situation of a people who did not see with clear eyes and denied a name, recognition and life. Long before you and I arrived on the scene, there was a young woman from a poor village who gave birth to a son. The world doubted and distrusted her son as a baby and as a man, as anything other than someone who merited death. Quite paradoxically to our culture today, it was this woman—the mother—who refused to deny his status. It was the mother who—in the face of immense opposition—demonstrated the strength of holding firm in her heart the gift and grace of life from the one and only maker of souls. While men cried out for death, it was this mother's actions that spoke volumes. It was Mary, under the cross, who stood firm and never lowered her eyes. It was Mary who faced the world and refused to deny a name. Truth can do that.

Jesus died that we may have life. We are commanded: Do not kill. Yet we killed the giver of all Life, and we continue to kill the life He gifts. Obviously we have learned very little.

Chapter
SIXTEEN

CHAPTER SIXTEEN

God paints His own portrait in the depths of our souls.
BROTHER LAWRENCE (1611-1691)

Have you ever had the experience of being in a crowded place but feeling invisible, as if you do not exist? Perhaps it was at a business function, a party, a shopping mall, or even at a family gathering. You were made to feel unimportant; non-existent; nothing. You were among many but awarded recognition by no one. That is the child you have tried desperately to ignore. That is your nameless child. That is the life you want to believe is not alive. There is another heart beating inside you. It is a heart counting on your legs to walk so as to rock it by day; counting on your hands to ensure that what feeds you will also nourish it; counting on your ears so it may become familiar with your voice; counting on your voice to give it a name instead of naming it a procedure. That heart beating is counting on a "yes" not a "no." Counting on a "yes." Not a "later." Not a "maybe." Not a "I'm not ready." Not "School is more important." Not "I cannot risk losing my boyfriend." Just a "yes." "No" seems like the easy answer. "No" seems like the best answer given the circumstances. If "no" is your answer know to whom your answer is directed. You are rejecting the highest of gifts from the highest of authority. Is your pro choice to silence this heartbeat born from ignorance or weakness? You will always be able to find a crowd that will make you feel invisible, and you will always be able to find a crowd deaf to whatever they do not wish to hear.

Your perception may be that it is "only tissue," but then your perception is without ears. Does not this tissue have a beat? Does a body live without a heart that beats? Is not a beating heart prerequisite to human life even if you insist on using the term "tissue?" Word games do not change truth.

If you believe your pregnancy to have been a "mistake;" the failure of contraception; the result of a fault not your own, then how do you explain the delivery of that soul. Did God make a mistake, too?

Instead of asking whose life it is, perhaps the question should be: Whose soul is it? Whose hand gives this soul? Whose hand dares to turn the cradle into a casket?

Who plants the soul? Would it be the same hand that formed the mountain and filled the sea? And, if so, would this planter of souls deliver death or life? The wild beasts know better than to act other than their innate instinct planted by this marvelous hand. For those who struggle to acknowledge a Divine hand, that struggle is certainly permitted thought. But permitted thought denotes nothing more than free thinking and free thinking that dismisses truth unveils an imprisoned mind and a man easily sold by clever marketing. Like a fish baited. With a spirit of perceived freedom one allows his thoughts to be taken off-road into dangerous territory without a map, a compass or a GPS.

When God created the world and everything in it, He could have made the earth bigger. He could have made smaller waters and larger land masses. He could have made fewer land animals and more sea creatures. He could have chosen for every human person to be placed on the planet at the same time. Our "time to live and time to die" could have been orchestrated to be the same date stamp. God created His way which is perfect. Then God did something even more mind-blowing, He willed that man should be co-creators with him. Notice the word: co-creators. Not co-destroyers. God is a God of life, not death. God loves intimacy. He demonstrated this fact by creating Adam; then seeing that Adam was lonely, created Eve from Adam. How intimate can you get? Do you not think taking the rib of one to make the other is intimate? God could have created an Adam and an Abe and an Alfred for that inaugural walk in the garden. Then seeing they yearned for more complementary company he could have made Eve, Elizabeth and Erica to accompany them. Instead, God chose intimacy. The beautiful gift of intimacy was specifically made to be between one man and one woman, with God. Intimacy is a duet with the orchestrator of all life; not threesomes of lust, use and dispose. Nor is intimacy men couplings or women couplings; true intimacy always honors the highest respect for the human person as originally designed. Animals do not have the gift of intimacy.

If we follow our creative design as God willed it to be, the only protection we shall ever need is protection from the evil that makes never-ending attempts to confuse what is right and feed our selfish egos for the want of variety. Such is the case that the grass might be greener in another pasture. It is a trap in which many are caught because they do not understand real love.

Mary, the Blessed Virgin, Mother of our Redeemer, conceived, brought forth and nourished Christ. It was an order of grace— a gift of grace—that the maternity of Mary began. Souls are graced; they are gifted—gifted by the one and only maker of souls. Have you heard the phrase: We were graced by her presence? Even the secular world knows this truth. They are just not always quick to give credit where credit is due, or, rather, to whom the credit is due. With all that we think of ourselves there is often little space left in our hearts or minds to think of anyone other than self. Saint John Paul II once said, "For it must be recognized that before anyone else it was God himself, the Eternal Father, who entrusted himself to the Virgin of Nazareth, giving her his own Son in the mystery of the Incarnation."

To conceive is a gift. It is a precisely chosen, planned, highly customized gift…Heaven sent. Did you not issue the invite or did you just not intend for the invite to be accepted? Do you not understand that no pharmaceutical company has the capacity to override Divine Providence? What then about this gift must you "protect" yourself? What about this gift needs to be recalled? What about this gift do you reject? What about this gift do you find so offensive that you must wage an interior war against it and yourself? God did not create us to use one another. He created us to love one another. And sexual intimacy is a pro-creative design and action. God's pro-choice is consciously planned with deliberate limitations that offer us the only protection needed—one man and one woman joined together in intimate, committed union.

We tend to think God got it wrong and when we make such an argument we argue with ignorance. It happens whenever you start thinking yourself center of the universe. You begin to believe that not only do you control your free will (which is true) but that you also have control of things and situations outside your free will (which is false). At this point the argument digresses into a demonstration of physical ignorance and mental foolishness. And while not an interesting argument, it is entertaining from the standpoint that the sun illuminates another day giving mankind yet another opportunity to learn the lesson that the more we know the less we know, and to acknowledge that the One who created us knows all, always.

Chapter
SEVENTEEN

CHAPTER SEVENTEEN

Changing definitions is hardly an honorable practice.

THOMAS DUBAY

What is it you want? A religious reason to be lazy? A free pass to skip this pregnancy with a promise to not abort next time? Irresponsible to relationships and indifferent to reality, is that the comfort you seek? What type of comfort would that be, really? Do you want a dead conscious to accompany your numb life?

Jesus asked those closest to him: Who do the crowds say that I am? Then he asked them: But who do you say I am? The crowds did not know what his friends knew. If Jesus stood before you, pointed to your newly pregnant womb and asked, "But who do you say is inside there," how would you answer him?

You have right to your thoughts, but you do not have right to the thoughts that grow within your womb. You have right to your voice, but the voice inside you begs time to speak for itself. You have right to your body, but ownership of your body lies in hands beyond your own. And life, which was so many years ago breathed into you, and which now has been breathed into another through you via the cooperative creative act of sexual intercourse, is a life entrusted to your defense and to your safe delivery. What you own is the responsibility to deliver the body entrusted to your care. The question is: Can God trust you to deliver?

Is it any wonder we kill? Did our freedom to choose not begin in a garden? Life is a radical gift. Only God has the goodness to bestow such a radical gift. Why? Because radical is release. It breaks chains; it relinquishes control—free will, love, sacrifice. We fight life. It is a battle we first waged in a garden. There was a tree of life. We were to let it be. One tree—a tree of life—was marked off limits to our interference. But, alas, under the banner of "pro choice" we ignored God and chose death. God gave life; Adam and Eve rejected life. Bad decision. And now we have taken their bad decision and raised the stakes. Under the pro choice flag we have broadened the scope of this death penalty beyond our own sentencing and blurred into oblivion all boundaries between right and wrong and condemned into extinction the body and soul of which we do not even possess. Who am I to tell you? That is not the question. The question is: Who are you to tell God? The question is not "How did this happen?" the question is "How could I believe this could not happen?" Sex is a creative encounter. It was meant to feel good just as it is when you unwrap a present from someone you cherish. If you do not understand love—real love—you will have a challenging time understanding sex and you will most seriously have tremendous difficulty—not to mention tremendous pain— understanding life. Life within you and life outside you but tethered to you. I sense many squirming as their eyes take up the print from these pages and their minds bat the words between their ears. Some may be agitated, but, again, it is not the author of this book with whom you have issue. The issue you have is with the Author of all Life. How will you come to see? How will you come to acknowledge life? I crave to give you the answer, but I can only help direct you to it. You alone decide whose plan is "pro" in your choice.

Modern society happily feeds our selfishness and crass independency. Our culture will grant—if not bless—every loathsome gratification we desire and any murderous ambition licensed. Modern society has declared war on its own heart. Our culture curses the person who is not pliable to its plans, and number one on the hit parade is the infant, unable to negotiate rent in the temporary housing of the womb.

We should not be questioning God; God should be questioning us. God knew us first. Do you know Him? Before it ever crossed our minds that God might be important, God singled us out as important. Our lives are not part of a scavenger hunt; our lives were not designed as puzzle pieces. I am not the center of the universe and neither are you, but our egos often work overtime in want of gaining the title. It is a downward spiraling career in the end.

We are not Lone Rangers no matter how proudly we may prance or how boastfully we may raise our voices and parade our treasures. Whenever one claims "I did it," what exactly was it they did? Who did they listen to in doing what they did? And whatever it was they did, tell me honestly: Was it not more than the solo act of their one-dimensional vision at work, either for good or for evil? Most of us are in need of an eye exam. There is a perfect plan for your life. It is one-of-a-kind and it is patented. It is a plan that only you can fulfill and if you "pro choice" not to, then it will forever be a plan aborted.

Some of us will occasionally drop into church simply to see what is happening with God. Some approach the thought of going to church as if under some type of a restraining order. Some react as if they have an allergy about all things "religious." Others of us elect to indulge in various "cafeteria" plans of worship; whatever has been discovered that speaks to them or, maybe better stated, whatever won't talk back.

The fundamental and recurring mistake is to start with ourselves instead of God. God is the alpha and the omega. We are in God's storybook. He wrote the beginning, the middle, and He has written the end. He has shared His storybook with us, but, just like spoiled actors, we want a rewrite of our part. Some want a bigger part, some a smaller part, always a different role—our will not His. As Dante said, "In His will, our peace." Even when you do not understand yourself, God understands.

We fight on behalf of the planet. We fight on behalf of our four-legged friends and all kinds of critters. We are Green people, we are PETA people, we are just not People people.

We are confused about what constitutes a person. We choose a bad history book and entertain that an ape can be a man or a man can be an ape as if every day is Halloween; as if every day is a masquerade ball. Pretending to be what we are not, not owning who we are. It is not a "what" we are; it is a "who" we are. We are a name.

This is an all-out moral battle. It is a matter of right and wrong with not one inch of space in the middle. You must stand on one side or the other, with the side of wrong in casket position. Each of us—you and me—most specifically, most personally, were born on the side of righteousness and good. How do I know? Because God proclaimed it to be, and He has been the only one from the beginning of time to keep His word. We either stay true to our calling and our original design or traitorously defect from it. You are not from your parents. You are from God. Think about that. God delivers you first. Then God entrusts you—depends on you—to do the right thing in carrying through with Phase 2 of His delivery plan; a delivery the world needs according to Him who is the one and only knower of the plan for that life. Are you beginning to sense at all the enormity of the gift you have been chosen to carry? God, in his pro choice, has chosen you to deliver. Anyone with sincere desire to change the world should understand that it is only through life that the world can be changed. The giving of life is the most natural of processes. Open your mind and see. The process is ordered; there is obedience, a rhythm, a routine, a security to the process. We count on the four seasons; we count on wheat sprouting in the fields; grapes ripening on the vine; fruit growing on trees. We count on the sun rising and the moon taking its place when the sun—and we—need to rest. We count on rain falling down not up. We count on wind blowing not suctioning. We count on forests giving shade and wells giving water. We count on cows giving milk and chickens giving eggs. We count on a man and wife, together, giving name to life; a name listed in Heaven with a mission they have been gifted and entrusted to deliver. This mission from God, should they decide to accept it, will change the world.

Chapter
EIGHTEEN

CHAPTER EIGHTEEN

The problem is not with the truth,
but aversion of the truth.
What is your sensitivity to truth?
The Pharisees shrugged off some things too,
but they have never been noted for authenticity.

Incalculable evil can initiate from the most unlikely sources in seemingly innocent ways. One way is through appeasement. Appeasement is often confused as bringing peace. You don't want to "rock the boat;" you are scared and do not want to "make waves." But soon you see you are on board the Titanic. The ship that was unsinkable sunk. The iceberg was immoveable, just like truth. When we go off course, it is wise to look to Heaven to get the proper coordinates. One voice—steadfast—can change the course of an event; whether a ship carrying many lives or a womb carrying one. The question is: Does the voice speak of right or wrong; truth or manipulation of truth? Your duty as a human person is to know right from wrong; truth from fallacy, and to pro choice what is righteous, not what is just right now, the fashionable stand of the moment. A virtuous life may not be popular in our secular society, but eternity does not require win of a popularity contest.

What is peace? How does one get peace? Peace or lack of peace is not an exterior phenomenon. Peace is inside work. Nothing—absolutely nothing—can cause disturbance to your interior peace without your authority. You must agree to the invite; you must accept the upset. With unclenched hands comes tranquility. As often as there may be things that transpire to present obstacles in our lives, we absolutely have control of our response. This is neither a new revelation nor a new message, but it seems to be something we think applies only to others. We like to think ourselves always as that one special exception; the one exemption. Envision your future. Where would be your ideal permanent home? Do several places come to mind or just one? Is it easy for you to think so many years ahead or does it make you uncomfortable to entertain the question? In giving thought about your ideal permanent home, did Heaven even enter your mind? If not, why not? Might it be that Heaven seems as far away from reality as you would wish the distance of the reality of the life inside you now? How badly you wish to slap a label as a Band-Aid on your situation. It is/was an accident; a mistake; tissue; not wanted now; a burden; unmanageable; in the way; a cramp in your style; the failure of birth control; unplanned. When truth speaks in answer to any of these labels, it speaks to the utter lack of self-control of two people—one male, one female. The only thing unplanned was the priority ordering of the purpose of sexual encounter. Sex is beautiful and sex feels good—very good, but sexual freedom is designed to be free and can only truly be free in a committed, life-long marital union, no matter how strongly you wish to express otherwise. Ask any unwed female of any age who finds herself with a positive pregnancy test how free she feels. Ask her then how "sexual freedom" is working for her. She may describe feeling used, rejected, frightened, alone, shameful, judged, trapped, helpless; she may feel any number of thoughts and emotions, but be assured she does not feel free. No girl, no woman, should ever feel this loss of freedom. It is unnatural. And anything that is unnatural does not come without pain; pain that is the result of revolting against the natural and the Divine.

We seem more concerned with smoothing things over than in making things right. No one ever wants to be the unpopular kid. And in today's world, many—so as not to be unpopular—have crowned a new leper. There is no one more unpopular than the unborn kid.

You want peace? How can you expect to ever have peace when you compromise what is right? How do I know what is right? I do not know, but God knows. His knowledge is without limit and His eyes without blind spots. I trust that as He went to the cross to be put to death at the hand of man, no man saw that to be pedestal to our salvation. You want peace? Then you have to touch the pain points. A doctor does not apply a Band-Aid to a broken leg. Why then should your dull senses override common sense? And, common sense, like it or not, says that humans birth humans. Peace will never come until we stop killing ourselves. To know truth you must know where Truth resides. Look at how Truth entered the world once for all. It was not a red carpet Hollywood entrance but it was a star search. Three Wise Men bowed to an infant while one evil king ordered the roundup and slaughter of hundreds of infants. Are we wise men or do we believe ourselves king?

Toothpaste: Once it is out of the tube can you put it back? No. Once words are voiced the sound is scattered, never to be retrieved and put back. You may have meant the words for only one set of ears, but you have no guarantee that other ears did not hear at least some quantity of your words. The simplest evangelization is your face greeting another each day. What does your face communicate? Smile or scorn? Pain or light? Peace or alarm? Comfort or unrest? Judgment or compassion?

This is not as simple as flushing a goldfish down the toilet, but we so badly want to believe it to be. We apply label after label until we find one that will stick without apparent sting, and when that label becomes thin we hunt quickly for another. We are proficient label makers; cover-ups extraordinaire. However, no matter the label, no matter the cover, some things cannot be silenced until they are given voice. And, in this case, there is no way around the fact you must speak for two; ultimately, both lives depend on it.

You are not alone. Let your ears clearly receive this truth: You are not alone. Shame is a heavy, destructive weight and I am aware of no one who escapes it in such circumstance. It can be buried, temporarily, but it will not release without face-to-face combat. Same goes if you are stuck in a blame game. Ultimately, in the case of "your body, your choice" the guillotine falls at your command. Pilate desired to wash his hands from the execution order of our Lord, but it is still Pilate's blood on the seal. There is but one fingerprint on the pen; one signature on the directive. Where is the soap to erase fingerprints? Where is the bath to make clean a murder?

Chapter
NINETEEN

CHAPTER NINETEEN

Secular philosophy is theology's handmaid.

SAINT CLEMENT OF ALEXANDRIA

Do you view your life as essential? Similar to the question the character George Bailey ponders in *It's a Wonderful Life*: What if you had never been born? Well, not only were you born, you were planned; planned by God. And such is the fallacy behind Planned Parenthood. God is our parent, and he did, in fact, plan each of us. You were chosen. I was chosen. Each of us is chosen. Your life, my life, every single human life is absolutely essential, absolutely. It is true: Your presence in the world is preciously mandatory. Why is this true? Because the one who planned, chose, and created you says so. Most concede the point that God created us. It is His timeline they wrestle with and dispute. At what time are we made? At what point do we become human in the womb? As I write this, I am laughing at the utter ridiculousness of the question. Do you not see the silly stupidity? It is like putting God on Jeopardy and thinking He could actually be stumped.

You claim to see, but refuse to acknowledge what is invisible. If you cannot see the flame of a candle does that mean the candle is not lit? Turn out the lights and you will have your answer. Do the stars hang in the sky only in the night or are they just not appreciated until darkness comes?

You claim to look but, in reality, you overlook. On one hand you choose to believe there is nothing to the invisible while on the other hand you spend a great deal of time and energy fighting all you cannot see.

Do you think I do not care to hear what you have to say? Do you believe I am trying to drown out your voice by virtue of my own voice? Neither is the case. I want to listen to all you have to say. It is not I who is not allowing someone a voice. It is not I drowning a voice. No, it is you dealing those cards. I want to hear what you have to say because God gave you a voice to be heard. Understanding and acknowledging this truth I also understand and acknowledge that your voice is meant to be in harmony with His, and, if that should not be, is it not my duty to recognize what voice may be speaking through you and gently bring it to your attention, not in judgment but in love; hoping that your ears may open to my voice as I, too, have been given something to say.

Therefore, the question I pose to you is this: Why do you not allow others to speak? What are you afraid of hearing? Is the voice inside your heart and the voice inside your womb not moaning loud enough for your attention? What is needed to remove the wax from your ears before you dispose of the life from your womb? Which of us is in need of hearing aid? I want to hear what you have to say and I also want to know what the life you house inside has been chosen to say and chosen to do.

Your so-called "progressive" thoughts are regressive in action, but you fail to see it because you are traveling in a backward movement. Therefore, it is motion-sickness that has confused your sense of right direction.

An empty womb is an empty house. When you invite a guest into your home, as you do through sexual intercourse, whether or not you have hired bouncers to stand at the door, you are— by truth—opening your home to a guest appearance. It is not acceptable in any natural or Divine realm to kill an invited guest.

Why are you forever restructuring situations and scenarios? Why do you insist on tilting your head for a more favorable view; begging for any blanket that can warm your mind to accept the unacceptable and kindly cause blindness to all your eyes never wish to see? Change the landscape as much as you dare, the answer sheet remains intact. When it comes to truth the answers are always unchanged; it is only the tap dance of refusing the answers that we hang ourselves in avoidance of what ultimately is unavoidable. Eternity is the irritant we will be brought to face.

Do you talk about God or do you talk to God? Prayer is not to be a caller request line; a one-way street where we speak and God takes notes. Isn't it interesting how God gave us free will and how he respects our free will? He waits to be invited into a conversation, into a home, into your work, into your life. He walks along side you everyday hoping to be noticed; longing to be called upon. He aches for the want to be of help. He thirsts for you. Do you know what that means? It is heartbreak. Our

Lord hung on a cross and gave everything—everything—so that we could live eternally. You and I cannot even begin to truly embrace the depth of such sacrificial love. We still think God holds out on us at times. We still think that God is out to "get us." God is out to get you, but not in a punishing way but in the most loving, forgiving, healing way.

So why do you avoid He who holds every answer? Is your schedule so full with other commitments that an appointment with God seems rather burdensome, if not truly unnecessary? Some will allow Him time on the clock, often to the likes of a 30-second buzzer. You want quick, fast, easy answers. Why do you find it so objectionable to put on your listening ears and park your ego? You cut Him off and then eventually cut Him out. God is not a puzzle and he is not a problem to be solved. God is our center. God is the answer, no matter what the question. We are made in His likeness; He came first.

Do you believe there is anything that God may have to say that might be worthy of your exclusive attention? If so, what might the topic(s) be? What if one of the topics in need of your undivided attention is a topic which you prefer to table? Table for later discussion; better timing according to your calendar. We have timetables; God has providence. When we pro choice against what is natural and then, with the same mouth, utter that we take God seriously, but… By issuance of the "but" we take most seriously self. Our life matters to us; every person's life matters to God.

Chapter TWENTY

CHAPTER TWENTY

A sense suggests; faith assures. What of the greatest of
our human insight is capable of judging the divine?

Is it not odd how we deny what was written on stone or what is etched in our soul, but we accept what is plastered on billboards or what is repeated by the largest crowds? The command of life does not restrict natural freedom it creates the conditions of freedom. What is your response-ability? Where is your sense of continuity? You are pleased to respond to whims, but you retreat when called to respond to truth. Amnesia is the friend in your con against life. But no matter the life you fail to recognize, that soul will never escape attention and care of the mind that planned it, the eyes that chose it, the hands that blessed and gifted it for you to defend and deliver.

You do not want to follow God but you will follow the crowd. You talk about rights and tolerance but you dehumanize the life growing within your womb. You parade against the wearing of fur and ingestion of animal flesh while you vilify those who march against the killing of the tiniest of human flesh. You use retorts such as it is "just tissue" and "not fully formed." You desperately need the comfort of any seemingly reasonable falsehood. Where is the soul? Has not a soul arrived with "the tissue?" Is it not the soul that transforms what some regard as "just tissue" to that of *a person*? If not, how is it that a heart starts? How is it that anything may develop from *just tissue* if that *tissue* is not life that has been gifted? Humans simply do not possess the ability to create the soul. What do I know? Why don't you ask God what He knows. I found my answer through Him.

Are you familiar with the prayer *Our Father*, also known as *The Lord's Prayer*? These specific words Jesus personally taught His disciples to pray. Do you find this prayer offensive? Is there anything about this prayer to which you disagree? Here is the *Our Father*:

> *Our Father who art in Heaven,*
> *Hallowed be Thy name;*
> *Thy kingdom come,*
> *Thy will be done on earth as it is in Heaven.*
> *Give us this day our daily bread;*
> *and forgive us our trespasses as we forgive*
> *those who trespass against us.*
> *And lead us not into temptation;*
> *but deliver us from evil.*
> *Amen.*

Do you believe this prayer to be of merit, value, goodness, and truth? Whose will should be done? Some would say it depends on the situation. Do not most of us subscribe to the false trinity of me, myself, and I? Is not my life my kingdom? Am I not ruler of me? The answer is: yes and no. For now yes; for eternity no. The quandary is that our now effects eternity.

Do you pray these words or simply parrot them? Do these words spill from your heart or evaporate once they spill from your mouth? It is whenever we become frustrated with God that our kingdom becomes preferable to "Thy kingdom." How easily are we frustrated?

Have you ever made a bad decision? Contrast whatever number of bad decisions you made in just the last year to the number of bad decisions made by God since the moment he uttered the job description of the sun and the moon and the stars. Is it not astounding whose kingdom we continue to trust and whose Kingdom we continue to question when declaring who is owner of one's body? There is no such game of doing some things by God's will and some things by our will. Anything against God's will is ultimately a choice against life…ultimately the side of the ground worm who speaks lies. Thy kingdom of self was, is, and will always prove to be a bankrupt kingdom, but we continue to try to prove otherwise. I call this fool proof.

Please draw your focus to the following lines:

> *Our Father who art in Heaven…*
> *Thy will be done on earth as it is in Heaven.*

Let's walk through these two lines, one at a time:

Our Father who art in Heaven…

Jesus teaches that God, our Father—his Father and our Father, resides in Heaven. Heaven is the home of God. God is at home in Heaven. So if Heaven is God's home that also is our home because we are a creation of God. God made us. Like Jesus, we are Heaven sent. You and I live outside of Heaven; therefore, we are not at home. It could be rightly said that we are living in exile because man was meant to live in union with God. When Eve got chatty with a snake and Adam failed to step up and confront the snake in defense of his wife, the free will of Adam and Eve went free-wheeling and put each and every one of us in a downward spiral. Ever since, that pro choice of the con requires daily recovery.

Thy will be done on earth as it is in Heaven…

In Heaven, souls live. Souls are not aborted; souls are celebrated. If God is the giver of souls, and God, being Our Father who art in Heaven, delivers the soul into the womb by power and authority of His Holy Spirit, then I beg you to answer His throne and tell him who you are to override His throne. It is called abortion of your own soul. Your will most evilly interrupting His will; and it is in direct opposition to what is proclaimed when you pray "on earth as it is in Heaven." I assume that you have heard the story (at least around the time of Christmas) of the angel who appeared to

Mary and spoke of God's desire for her to bear His son. With her fiat (aligning her will to Thy will of God) she was overshadowed by the power of God's Holy Spirit and was then immediately "with child."

Mary's pregnancy was not immediately visible to others just as no woman's pregnancy is immediately visible to others. Conception is not announced by what the human eye is able to conceive, but by what the Divine eye is able to conceive. Your Guardian Angel knows and the Guardian Angel of the soul inside the womb knows.

We think we are taking a risk when we choose to listen to God. We somehow think it is our voice that is infallible or at least speaks the better plan. Perhaps this is because we never shut up long enough to hear any voice other than our own, or because we do not remove ourselves away from the crowd to a place where we can hear truth whisper. To believe God a bad risk and ourselves a good risk is virtual insanity if not masochism. Without God we walk blindly through an undeniable land mine.

Chapter
TWENTY-ONE

CHAPTER TWENTY-ONE

Do you stand with the world
or the One who made it?

For anything to work well there must be order. I trust you have heard the phrase: Too many chefs in the kitchen. That is society today; everyone throwing ingredients into the pot with no one bothering to check the recipe. Everyone thinking he knows exactly what is best when, in fact, he has never actually made the dish. There is a master chef who created the recipe and wrote a book giving full instruction, but the crowd in the kitchen is opinionated and loud. They resist order because they tend to view obedience as weak.

Is not the secret to a great, strong military order and obedience? Is not the secret to winning a war order and obedience? I dare suppose no soldier would pro choice to share a foxhole with anyone not committed to order and obedience because it is life that is on the line.

When you abort what is in the womb, you self-elect insubordination to the supreme order of life rather than rise to the level of power required to deliver. Feminists fought for the right to participate in active duty of all branches of the military, yet, for all that effort, the feminists are proving they are not at all up to the task of what is first and primary to military service—subordination to order and submission of will in obedience to order. If a woman will not go to battle for her infant, it is highly and seriously suspect to believe she is capable of combat. There simply is no greater conflict than interior conflict. There simply is no greater struggle to overcome than fighting to save the life of another; above all, the life of another of which you are co-creator. It is a reenactment, if you will, of Jesus on the cross. God chose not to abort us.

We pro choice to lose and blame God for our loss. We pro choice the great con: evil. It is the job of evil to twist words, manipulate circumstance, and chip away instructions that were written in stone. To play wildly on the field of subtlety, to turn complex what was made simple, to separate and divide all that was designed to be joined and united. There is a proper order to life and it necessitates obedience.

If we do not accept that it is a child from the very beginning of the nine-month countdown, then how is it that it becomes a child at any point in the countdown? Is not an acorn an acorn tree? Just because your eye is unable to behold the fullness of the tree does not rob the truth that the fullness exists and is clearly in the sight of the One who created the seed. The human seed is the soul. The soul announces the arrival of a Heaven-sent gift to earth. How unbelievably beautiful; how incredibly astounding this gift. Do you accept this truth? You must choose pro or con; there is no middle ground. There is no neutral to truth. Evil says "no" to life but it frames it with a "pro" so that it sounds positive instead of evil. God says "yes" to life and God says "yes" to free will. God trusts that you will trust Him. Your free will is singular; it does not overflow to the free will of the heart that beats within your womb. That heartbeat was set into motion by God and it has not been given to you to stop.

Our culture has declared war on its own heart. Our culture curses the person who is not pliable to its plans. The person who resides in a womb we prefer reside in a tomb. Does it matter then how pretty we attempt to make everything appear on the outside if it is the core that is rotten?

Did the Lord Jesus Christ appear in Mary's womb an 8 lb. 2 oz. baby boy at the moment of conception? No. It took nine months, exactly as God Almighty designed the seed of life to begin and to develop. It is not *just tissue*; it is life—human life. There is not a window of opportunity to destroy nothing; only a window of opportunity to destroy someone. And, truth be told, it is impossible to kill the seed inside the womb without also inflicting a mortal wound on the parents of the seed. It is we who are made in the likeness of God. God did not fashion himself to be in the likeness of us. And just as Jesus was immediately present and alive inside His mother's womb, our arrival and real presence in the womb is never, and can never be, DOA. Life is conceived; death cannot be conceived. It is not by measurement of the body; it is by measurement of the soul. Arrival of a whole human being is not delayed even one second on God's watch. Motherhood and fatherhood instantly become your crown whether you pro-choice your child to a cradle or, by force, to a casket. And the reason this is so is because while you wrongly may wield your free will to manic proportion, you can never destroy what God alone renders ultimate judgment: the soul. The one-of-a-kind meticulously planned, chosen, necessary, and loved person that God most personally created. It matters not if that soul inside your womb housed for one minute, one day, or one month; in the first second of its arrival your name forever changed. Mother. Father. Your child knows your name for eternity. The question is: Will you give name to your child?

People try to be good without God but that does not work. Some think it a waste of time to pray without considering that it could be time not spent in prayer that is most profoundly wasted. How can God give when we are not willing to listen, and, even more, we are unwilling to receive what He gives? Adam and Eve accused God of holding out on them in the Garden; it seems many of us still hold to the same accusation. Who, honestly, is holding out on whom? You argue that you have prayed for certain things and nothing has happened; but how do you know nothing has happened. Is it not true that you, being human, are subject to tunnel vision and a limited mode of operation? Is it not true that God, being Divine, is without limitation? Is it that nothing has happened or is it that nothing has happened that is to your liking? Remember, we are not the only ones with free will. It is wise to understand—and even wiser to act upon the knowledge—that the last and final word is reserved for God. A good life can never come to pass outside of alignment with He who created everything, knows everything, and gives everything that is good.

Have you really discarded faith? If so, you do not give thought to the sun rising day after day, as if any scientist can make it so, or any seat in Congress or any borrower of the Oval Office. Is it self-faith you have? Is your religion the sports schedule, shopping, drugs, alcohol, pornography, work, or the tech cloud? Whatever you choose to be servant, is that not your religion? Religion is not servitude but love in service. Religion that we make-up as we go along so as to not offend anyone about anything reduces us to the hell of insiders in a pee-wee existence. It is a trivial and stunted life. We like to manipulate because we want control. The larger the world the less of it we can subject to our own architecture: I want this job; I want to make this salary; I want to meet this person; I want to have this car, this house, this vacation; I want to retire at this age; I want…I want…I want. Then your days run out and you realize the question that was in need of answer was not what did I get but what did I give?

I assume you have heard it said, "Divide and conquer." Pro choice failure to deliver the child and you divide and conquer the family. Conquer the family and you divide and conquer the greatest of nations on this earth.

Creation was made to work—work well—and what is part of creation matters; it has importance. Your soul matters to the whole of creation and without your soul in the whole there is, in the natural and in the supernatural, a hole. We are one family because from One we have all come. Free will, alone, breaks the connectors. Let us not exploit, nor judge, nor reject, nor exclude. Let us love. Love is our mission, our calling. Love is our creation and the purpose of our form. So let us love and then let us trust that God will battle everything else. Love is a tall order; it quite literally and figuratively rises above all else. It rises not in pride but in humility. It rises not in arrogance but in humor of one's own acknowledged shortcomings.

The world in which we live is real, and the realities of this world are not to go without our close attention. But there is another reality in need of even greater attentiveness, and this reality is the reality we will each experience the very moment our body stills. One's soul will soar or it will steal away. Let us not connect ourselves to the feeding tube of lies but to the feeding tube of truth and life.

Chapter
TWENTY-TWO

CHAPTER TWENTY-TWO

Freedom is not the ability to release
your inhibitions and indulge in lustful behavior.
The person enslaved to lust is only as "free"
as an alcoholic who celebrates the fact
he can get drunk whenever he wishes.

UNKNOWN

We chase sex like we will die without it and then say things such as, "Oh, it's just sex," as if it holds no meaning whatsoever. We try to make sense but fall short of good sense because we have not employed the wisdom and order of God who designed the proper workings of sex. You can use someone and call it love, but love without God isn't true love. Our culture wants to treat living together as normal and waiting for marriage as abnormal. Sex is not wrong and it is not dirty, but without God it is empty. People say they love the Lord, but then they go do whatever it is they want to do.

When a man and a woman choose to live together they are electing convenience and use over love. The problem with their array of reasoning is none of it includes God's wisdom. In today's hook-up, shack-up, toss-out society, it requires tremendous tenacity not to join the stampede; tremendous faith not to sign-up for membership in the culture club of counterfeit. What exactly is it about another person that you need to "sample before purchase?" Might the problem be you? And if another allows free samples, why buy when you can lease for a period or rent month-to-month? It is crass but this is how we address relationships today. A familiar defense for delaying marriage is: We don't need a piece of paper; a piece of paper won't change how we feel. This is a correct statement. A piece of paper cannot change how one feels but it can change how one acts. Of course none of the "anti-paper" couples ever envision their love ending but neither do they envision it starting. The couple truly in love will never hesitate to make official by word and action their commitment to each other and to the world: Real love cannot wait to put it all on the line.

The list of "advantages" for living together can be touted and spread as thick or thin as one dares to paint but it remains a situation without authentic buy-in. It is simply a mentality that leaves God behind; and God—in a single word—is Love. "Living together"—faking committed relationship—we want not only to be acceptable, but acceptable and normal. God says lies and truth can never marry. Is not the umbrella of "benefit" for living together mostly self-serving advantage from association? What is not rooted is weak. We are made in the likeness of God but we want to re-shape ourselves…and to be what and like whom? By whose voice are we in tune when we go against our original form? We see and hear so many different things that prompt us to change, but change from what to what? It is easy to pull anchor and drift here to there; to vacillate. It is easy to let our eyes become intoxicated with external sights, forgetting the beauty inside thirsting to develop. Each of us is formed from the inside out, but when bowed to anyone other than God, we rot from the outside in. Culture, government, the local mob, or the one who made you and chose you: To whom do you bow? We are not self-made.

Chapter
TWENTY-THREE

CHAPTER TWENTY-THREE

Christianity came into history as a fact.
It was and is the fact of a new life
given by God through Christ
and in the name of Christ.

YVES CONGAR, 20TH CENTURY THEOLOGIAN

If I sound moralistic and if that leaves a bad taste in your mouth, to what do you attribute the disintegration of your taste for the best and finest life offers?

We shift between believing things cannot get any worse or things cannot get any better. We do not believe in hope just as we do not believe in judgment. We do not believe in the invisible hand of Love, only the visible hand of use. We don't believe in a Divine plan, only our self-designed control. Some do not believe much and some do not want much to believe.

We have more anxiety about what people think of us than what we think of our own actions, and almost no anxiety of what God may think.

Acts of hope are always sufferers to ridicule because they seem so outside of practicality. Human vision barely trusts visible reality; invisible reality is a near mindblower. Hope is not a wish. A wish is want in need of a backbone. A wish is want without committing any part of your life to making what seems impossible possible. Hope is an act. It is an act with conviction that God will complete the work underway even when—especially when—all evidences suggest differently.

Politicians want our hope but what can they give specifically to us that will uniquely and personally prove to be of pure goodness in result? Hope is putting it all on the line with trust in the outcome. The most practical thing we can do in life is to listen to what God says. The most common sense thing we can do in life is to listen to He who is Master of Common Sense. In a culture that demands instant everything it is not easy to act in hope because most of the immediate evidence is against it. We live in a country where the impractical overrides the practical and the practical overrides the supernatural. Or, stated another way, where spineless overrides courage. It takes courage to act in hope.

When someone says, "Oh, yes, that's a Biblical argument," that is a great opportunity to point out that God pre-dates the Bible, by a lot; as does Jesus and as does the Holy Spirit. God's actions spoke volumes long before they were recorded and published. The Bible, as with all other incredible gifts from God, was given to us to help. God has no need to be a best-selling author.

God does not have a "delay send" restriction when He breathes life into a soul. God delivers life. It is that beautiful, that fantastic, that simple, and that true. If you do not choose to believe it, you are likely still in the mindset of being owner of your body; unwilling to explore the deeper seat of grace.

To whom do you go when you want advice? By who are you influenced? Would you be more inclined to listen to someone who has general interest in you, or someone who has particular interest in you? Does the pharmaceutical company have a general interest in you or is it your pocketbook to which they are most attracted? Does the "unplanned" parenthood clinic have a particular interest in you or is it the general message of the crowd they wish to pacify by their softened spine. I may not know you, but I know your Father. He loves you passionately. God promises and he delivers on every one of His promises. He never fails—ever. Ask yourself, who else in your life has never failed you? There is only One, and He is waiting with open arms to welcome you back to His care.

When you don't feel godly you certainly don't want to go to church. I understand. But do you want to go to God? Do not let a bad experience keep you from the highest experience. Christianity is a religion of surrender. You are not the savior, Jesus is. Relax into His arms. He does not expect you to do this, or anything, by yourself.

The North Star has long been the guide for travelers on land and sea, keeping them accurately on course. But these travelers had to know, and be able to identify, the star in order for it to be of help. It is the same with God.

When we cannot make something beautiful we make it big. We were not born in a crowd, nor will we die so. Why then should we live as if accountability can be transferred upon a crowd? Crowds will turn every which way on a rumor and at the drop of a hat. The crowd turned on Jesus, and who do you think you are? Do not believe your own press—good or bad—especially when authored by a crowd.

You see your body every day. When was the last time you took a look at your soul? One day the seen will be unseen and the unseen will be seen. Do you believe this? Or does it tire your brain to ponder the thought? Will you fail to engage yourself in the work of your future?

We interpret to our own perverse inclination, although we would hardly agree we are inclined to such a direction. When we make right wrong and wrong right, in what direction have we oriented? We like to mix and match various devotions; shopping, if you will, for a belief we can buy. And it truly is a buyer's market with any variety of outlets that will happily justify immoral behavior asking only the price of body and soul.

If you do not want God now, why would God think you would want Him forever? Do you think God is surprised by anything you have done? Do you think that Jesus dying on the cross was not enough? Do you think that there is no hope for turning your life in a better direction? Well, think again. God has not given up on you; God longs for you. He wants you to get to know Him just as he already knows all about you. There is nothing—zero, nada, zilch—that you can do to stop God from loving you; only you can stop loving God

Chapter
TWENTY-FOUR

CHAPTER TWENTY-FOUR

Hope is reliance upon grace in the face of death:
the issue is that of receiving life as a gift,
not as a reward and not as a punishment.
Hope is living constantly, patiently,
expectantly, resiliently, joyously in
the efficacy of the Word of God.

WILLIAM STRINGFELLOW

Some question whether there is a God. Others believe there is a God but question what has been recorded about what He said, what He did, and what He really may have meant. If you think the visible world is all there is to your story, I appreciate your belief even though I do not share your belief. I will not choose to argue with you—or anyone—about whether God means what He says and says what He means. I will choose, however, to be out of control under His control.

Why do you choose to be out of control of your self-control? Why do you choose to stay in bondage of your anger? Why do you choose to be ruled by demons; although you know them by the softer, gentler term "addiction?"

It does not matter how high you jump, it matters only how straight you walk once you come down.

You want what God has but are not much interested in who God is. When you don't get the stuff you want you whine and pout. Does not friendship require self-disclosure? Part of God's self-disclosure you have laid on the table to abort. You want something better not seeing that the best offer is already on the table. You worry that the current situation will impede gain of a new job or the new boyfriend, so you sacrifice the new creation. You put a hard stop to life because you wrongly think you own it. You make the worst trade—body and soul—but who dares tell you? Be not afraid of Truth; only be afraid of failure to hear, listen, and act according to Truth.

When you "pro choice" what is it you are choosing that is lasting? If we cannot see beyond the horizon we fail to see what lasts. What have you chosen that is not dust? Is it ownership of your body or ownership of your soul that you claim? Whose will do you desire to serve: Your will or God's will? Will you surrender to life or to death? Something must die within each of us; however, it is not the gift of life given to be killed but the cunning evil that sees no gift inside that must be spotlighted and buried. Do you not yet see that although you now reside outside your mother's womb, you have always resided within God's spiritual body?

Because you do not see how your life can go on well, you invite death to end a child's life. Truth begs that you cover your ears to any convincing which may be motivated by the messenger's own weakness, anxieties, or failings. Seek the Word of He who holds your best interests in hand for a whole life; an eternal life. Hear His Word and you will no longer have cause to panic, only cause to persevere. Choose life for love of your soul, the gift of the soul wholly alive within your womb, and for love of Jesus who gave all and gives all—always without fail. There is absolutely no need to worry about your future unless your future does not include God; as there is simply no future for anyone without Him.

It is difficult to surrender. Even as we wildly protest that we own our bodies, we ache to drop into arms of unwavering resolve to carry us through. God knows every detail of your life; that's both the good and bad part you struggle with. You try again and again to escape where there is no escaping. You can only run so far, so long, to nowhere. God always knows where to find you. And with great and loving patience He waits as you struggle through your charade.

How large is the I-world in which you hide? How large is the secret you conceal? Life can only be as large as your smallest, most shameful, most fear-filled secret. You can bury your secrets, but then your secrets will bury you. If, however, you plant yourself in the light of truth what then can be your harm? What can "they" say or do to cause injury once you have shed the snake skin of your secrets and fully owned your every action spurred by your every choice? No one can hurt what stands naked in illumination of truth—whole and claimed. But it is a hard stand. We do not want our I-world upset. It seems easier to reject God, whom we do not see, than to reject the crowd, whom we do see. Therefore we barricade ourselves from whatever might expose our prejudices, or from people who challenge our narcissism. We mock as wacko and dispose as garbage any suggestion that we transcend biological comforts and psychological securities. We draw people around us—a crowd around us—as small as the thinking in our I-world.

We seek coziness not character. But how cozy can a casket be? Do you think life ends in a casket, or could there be more even before the dust has settled?

The "pursuit of happiness" is not prefaced with the words "quick" or "easy" or "comfortable," nor, I think, would the "pursuit of God" be prefaced. Why? Because God expects a lot. He expects a lot from us because He gave everything to us, and He knows that—with His daily help—we can actually meet His expectations (and exceed any and all of our own self-expectations). We have such distorted thoughts about God because we think so little about Him. Too many of us have little more than a stranger relationship with our Heavenly Father. So we pin him as mean; or someone who gets a thrill in "making us pay;" or "teaching us a lesson;" or any number of task master criticisms we can conjure to put in His mouth and imagine rolling off His tongue. Do we no longer hear the words of Jesus from the cross: "Father, forgive them, as they know not what they do."

While you continue to inventory everything you own; might it not be wise to flex your neck backward, lift your eyes upward, and ask how much "up there" you own? The truth of our behavior is rash self-confidence and self-indulgence by choice of ignorance unleashed as use of others driven by fear and shame. All here are followers. There is only one true Leader. Some will follow the crowd, some will follow their tail, and who dares follow the cross?

Each of us has prescribed limits: a time to be born, a time to live, a time to die; and it is a prescription issued by God's will. What name, then, is called the one who would abort the post assigned to another by God? What size is the unseen cemetery we have dug? How many children buried before we reach our fill?

It's not about being Holier than Thou; it's about being Holier than yesterday.

TWENTY-FIVE

Chapter
TWENTY-FIVE

CHAPTER TWENTY-FIVE

The moderate man is the invaluable
understrapper of the wicked man.
You, the moderate man, may be used for wrong,
but you are useless for right.

HERMAN MELVILLE

It is interesting how those who "pro choice" see themselves as taking positive control of a situation. But is it control or is it surrender? Surrender to killing. It has to be said that bluntly because the fact of the choice is so. It cannot be life later without being life right now. It would be a tough campaign to rally in favor of the slaughter of children. Therefore, so-called brilliant minds have taken to dummying down our language and dummying us down with their propaganda. The feminists are thrilled that scientific intellectuals concur the act to be "a procedure." It matters not that "the procedure" kills a child; it matters only that there be placed a period at the end of the word "procedure" and the file closed. "Procedure" is a generic enough term to provide reasonable cover-up for unreasonable minds doing evil. Cunning like the "control" feminists so badly seek and actually think they will find.

Explain the mind that believes peace will come to life by tearing any life to pieces. Yet, this is precisely what the feminists endorse for women, and it is the biggest con on women in our culture and in our world. The "pro choice" groupies are controlled by their own lack of self-control and their insatiable appetite for doing all they please in their I-world fueled by the dummying down ranks with whom they draw membership. And for a group who does exactly as they please with "their" body, it is amazing how angry they come across. Hostility escorts confusion. Peace escorts truth.

Do you think I can change your mind? No, I cannot change your mind. Only you can change direction of your thoughts and your actions.

To what school of thought do you desire to enroll: human or Divine? You certainly have familiarity with part of the story, but the question is do you have understanding of the whole of the story? Truth cannot be sectioned and still be labeled truth. Dissecting truth to ascertain a portion palatable to your taste is an elaborate exercise to stump a fool. Expand your appetite for truth and discover what is above human doubt and surpasses human reason. Be assured the discovery never gets old; it is always new, always fresh, always rewarding.

If it is true that the heart is the seat of the soul, and the heart announces life by its beat, then does it not follow that your pro choice to expel this seat and quiet this beat is a direct attack and tearing of heart strings—child from mother, mother from God? God on one end, mother on the other, a child connected by a cord meant only for cutting after delivery into loving arms. Those who choose their beliefs from a cafeteria plan instead of God's one perfect plan are the same about whom it can be said do not receive, by faith into their soul, the union of God and man.

When the foundation of the contention claims "ownership" of body, we are not only fighting a losing battle but a battle that was waged between human and angel—fallen angel. Dazzled by our self-proclaimed intellect we remain dazed. Just because we deem ourselves qualified assigners of names, and give rename to what has already been named as it pleasures us, does not give authority to our pleasure. As long as you choose to set aside truth in favor of giving air time to deceitful words and pointless speculation you will remain captive to the character of your own school. You may choose to name whatever you wish, as you wish, but until you dare decide to name what is true, your life and your life's future, will wrestle and squirm and weaken.

And should you believe that a troop of baboons once swung from a branch on your family tree, let me just say how I appreciate the entertainment behind such incredibly creative bridges which a mind can construct and clear, proving just how little narrow minds mind gaping holes.

Chapter
TWENTY-SIX

CHAPTER TWENTY-SIX

Although he was a son, he learned
obedience from what he suffered.

HEBREWS 4:15

Is there anyone in your life from whom you could learn nothing? Or might it be that you simply do not wish to know what they offer to teach. You prefer to teach. You prefer the speaking role over the listening role, not understanding all that you do not know. Wisdom comes through learning and learning comes from listening, witnessing and asking questions. The more we come to know the more we will understand all the more there is that we should come to know. Who are the teachers in your life and from whom did they learn? What is not rooted is weak.

Is your most pressing question, "What's in it for me?" Do you think Jesus did all that great stuff on the cross so He could go to Heaven? No, that sacrifice He gave for love of your life. He gave very personally for you. Jesus wants life for you, abundant and eternal. He asks that you make room in your life for Him and He asks that you make room in the womb for life. If anyone's life is diminished, every life is diminished. It is not for me, you, or anyone to defend God; God was not losing the battle when we entered the picture and God will not be in jeopardy of losing the battle once we exit. Only we are in danger of losing the battle. Might a good question be: Will we continue to pro choice the con on truth or not?

Few people are truly evil, but too few premeditate goodness. Goodness is not magic; it does not "just happen." Goodness requires intent, obedience, discipline, nurture, commitment and development over time. Few have the patience, the humility, the faith, or the stomach. Too many people in today's culture prefer to be formless; not desiring to declare anything right or wrong, negative or positive. They choose to be nothing in the middle hoping only to be surrounded by applause.

You only have now to live. You lived yesterday and tomorrow is not yours to claim. Now is the only space you have to mold; now is the only moment in anyone's life that is actionable. The free will choice you and I have in the "now" is to be active or to be inactive. And beware: inactive can camouflage as action as in the case of apathy where you surrender mindful thought to the mindless mob mentality. We all do it to some extent and to some regularity but, being aware, we can begin to do better.

To live successfully is to act in the now better than the moment just past. To live successfully is to be aware of our human limitations while, likewise, being aware that God has a specific plan for each of us. We need only stop fighting He who wants victory for us. We need only stop drawing lines of self-defense.

We need only turn from the emptiness of self-protection as we do not possess strength enough for the task. Pain is not God's plan for our life. Pain is the free will ingredient we pro-choice to sprinkle into our own day.

Engaging our minds before engaging our bodies would save untold heartache and pain. Active thinking instead of mindless submission would give your body a good lead. Focus on the highest good—that being God—will make us much less inclined to fall for the lower standards of man. Free will can bring any of us to our knees if our eyes fatigue from looking up.

Chapter
TWENTY-SEVEN

CHAPTER TWENTY-SEVEN

Never be afraid to trust an unknown future
to a known God.

Corrie Ten Boom

❧

Do you think God is bossy? How do you think we look to Him? Are we not officious?

Is God to blame for your situation? Is God responsible for the problems in your life? Are you angry with God? How is that working for you?

God is not your problem. Fear is your problem. Fear is the arm of defiance. Fear is a rebel of discord. Fear is poison that paralyzes. Fear is a wall that imprisons. Fear is a choice to stand still with the invisible who rules the darkness instead of moving with the invisible who rules the light. If only we would understand that the light of Heaven is always on, and it is darkness we invite by yielding to fear. Shame, guilt, embarrassment and bad behavior are all shadows under the umbrella of fear.

Fear is like dressing your soul with goods from Canal Street because you do not see how you could ever pull off wearing anything better.

Our Lord says, "Be not afraid" and He says it repeatedly. Do we hear Him now? When a bad decision is made, is it not fear that is the responder? Response to fear is distrust. It is a response as old as Adam and Eve. They were conquered and expelled from Paradise because they distrusted God. They chose to put their faith in words from a serpent. In fear they exercised pro-choice of the con and lost everything. God knew what was best but they were confronted with what seemed— from their eyes and to their ears—a better plan. This one man and this one woman chose death for their bodies, as well as for ours. Indeed, it was the first abortion. The short-changer they then learned was (and is always) the one looming in the dark. Adam and Eve chose night vision instead of the light of God's vision.

Fast forward to today and ask yourself: Why is it that we do not think it is death to perform "a procedure" that is, in every way, in opposition to God's plan for life? Our Lord has already told us over a hundred times: Be not afraid. God never fails to look upon us with love. We would be wise to stop looking at Him with an evil eye.

Chapter
TWENTY-EIGHT

CHAPTER TWENTY-EIGHT

As long as matters are really hopeful,
hope is mere flattery or platitude.
It is only when everything is hopeless
that hope begins to be a strength at all.
Like all the Christian virtues, it is as
unreasonable as it is indispensable.

G.K. CHESTERTON

When presented the question, "What is wrong with the world?" G.K. Chesterton responded, "I am." In his observation of the ills of the world he stated the world not to be unreasonable; rather that it is "nearly reasonable, but not quite." Indeed, it only takes a slight opening to let in a ray of the sun or a hungry termite. We teeter between ownership of our actions without implicating the body and ownership of our body without implicating our actions. We fear that if we tell the truth we may no longer be loved or wanted. It is hard for us—having the split personality between right and wrong—to trust that our wrongs committed can ever be forgiven, especially by the One who never did one thing wrong. How is it we may ever be seen as acceptable or loveable? Easy: Through the eyes of Love. Our Lord has the eyes of Love and it was these eyes that saw our face before the world, these eyes that saw our face from the cross, and these eyes that want to draw us to Him in Heaven. All that is needed is a contrite heart. All that is needed is to acknowledge the wrong and ask for His help to do what is right going forward.

Our Heavenly Father does not ask that we build Rome in a day. He asks that we place a single brick today. Tomorrow is groundwork for another brick. He knows what we can handle. Remember the words of The Lord's Prayer… "Give us this day…" He does not ask us to pray for the week; just this one precious day—now. Whenever we lament about the past or sweat about the future we cannot be present to the presence of now. Life is doing right or wrong in the moment.

Whom are you trying to please? Yourself? The father of "the tissue" or the Father of the soul? What are you trying to undo? What are you choosing to sacrifice? What is the price of silver you have set? If the situation is all too big for you, that is okay—be not afraid; it is not at all too big for God. May we not just profess to be of help, but be proven to be helpful. We always have a choice. In every situation we have a choice. It is only when we do not like the options that we claim to have no choice. Choosing right often falls into such a category.

I understand bad choices. I have made untold bad choices in my life. It is precisely in difficult situations that we must fight to not sever ourselves from Truth, no matter how challenging and uncomfortable truth may be to face. In choosing between right and wrong—based not on our wisdom but God's wisdom—we are choosing between life and death: our life or our death. By a thousand injuries, doing wrong is an abortion of its own type. Let us not abort what is good to be broken and made slave by what is evil. Let us not abort because we are scared to name. Let us be steadfast to confirm a safe delivery for each and every soul waiting for a name so that we may honor the name we were given before our face was visible to the visible. Let us not be silent to the truth, and when we speak let it be with the greatest of affection, compassion, and mercy.

Afterword

Before I formed you in the womb
I knew you,
before you were born
I dedicated you,
a prophet to the nations
I appointed you.

Jeremiah 1:5

AFTERWORD

Get a scroll and write…
Maybe the community…will finally get it…
JEREMIAH 36: 2-3 (MSG)

Jesus shares with us the real-life event of a woman who committed adultery. The Pharisees—self-righteous and with a supportive audience—rendered judgment against the woman believing the eyes of their human nature saw with the same clarity as the Divine eyes of God. Every person in that crowd held a stone—whether in their hand or in their mind—all were ready to kill the sinner.

The crisis of life and love in this account was adultery. The crisis of life and love to which I address today is abortion. Are you holding a rock?

I held a rock. The first time I picked up a rock was in my early 20s when I formed a definitive picture in my mind's eye of "that woman." That unspeakable woman who could do the unspeakable: kill her child. I could hardly comprehend the image of such a weak, miserable, ugly failure of a human being. The second time I picked up a rock was 17 years ago when I rode to an appointment that terminated a life. That woman knew she needed a safe, trusted ear to listen; a kind shoulder on which to lean; and a helping hand with a helpful plan. Her need was unmet; and, despite my convictions to the contrary, when the moment of truth arrived, my silence, too, was deadly.

It is so easy to judge, and simpler still to extend advice without extending action that could prove life-saving. Please think about it. Are you approachable? How would you assist someone pregnant and afraid? What if she was your unmarried daughter? Sister? Friend? Acquaintance? Stranger? Would you open your ears? Would you open your arms?

Would you open your home, with a seat at your table? Would you befriend the woman start to finish? Would you provide financial resource? Would you really? Who of us can truly be certain if we haven't been given the test? I was certain; then I failed. Just how far would you travel? I traveled to the doctor's office. I did not take hold of the woman's hand and help transform the weighty stone around her neck into a beautiful necklace. Seventeen years ago. Where is that woman today? Could I be of help to her now, or is she not deserving of help? She destroyed her baby, so should we slay her with our judgment; throw stones? Jesus saw that there was still a life to rescue; a life to love.

I understand this is a sensitive topic. It is its very sensitivity that renders it vital not to keep hidden in the disgrace of darkness but to shine on it the light of hope. Immense shame, guilt, fear, desperation, and isolation assail these women; our love is a necessary prescription. I stand in judgment of no one. I hold no honor in admitting that I have held rocks and that I have thrown rocks, most especially because the woman I knew who had the abortion that day was me.

I humbly ask that you consider what you hold in your hand, and do whatever necessary to ensure it is not a rock, but only love—love for your life and love for all those lives you come in contact, whether on the front end of this issue or the ever-after end. Let us start here, and, please, let us start now.

JEREMIAH . . .
God's prophetic bulldog
for our time.

Jeremiah was directed:
"Get a scroll and write... Maybe the community of Judah
will finally get it, finally understand the catastrophe that
I'm planning for them, turn back from their bad lives,
and let me forgive their perversity and sin."

JEREMIAH 36: 2-3 (MSG)

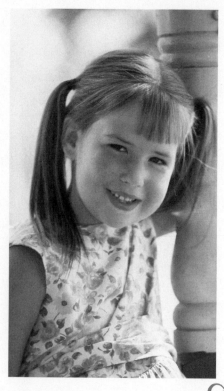

About
the author

Cynthia P. Cerny is published author of several books, including the best-selling *Losers, Creeps, Jerks & Weirdos: A Dating Story*. With refreshing transparency, the hallmark of her writing and speaking, Cynthia continues to appeal to, and attract, an ever-broadening audience of men and women, all ages, all circumstances. A long-time resident of Colorado, Cynthia spent over twenty years in the corporate world as the right-hand "man" to presidents, CEOs, and chairmen of boards. Compelled to write, Cynthia draws from her own experiences to reach out to others, bringing a message of hope, inspiration, and healing.

From "entertaining and humorous" in *Losers* to "inspirational and hopeful" in *Luna Tides* to "a work bound to change your life" in *What About Love?*, Cynthia's writing has been described as profound, genuine, and masterful, although she will tell you she is simply "a typist."

In addition to being a CCD kid and a graduate from the School of Hard Knocks and Slow Learners, Cynthia attended the University of Denver. She is dedicated to sharing a simple, practical message of truth and empowerment for women and men. Cynthia understands that sometimes we are afraid to learn what our gut already knows, but cautions that what you deny does not disappear, and always ~ always ~ actions trump words.